John Rae

The Statutes of Henry VII.

In Exact Facsimile, From the Very Rare Original, Printed by Caxton in 1489

John Rae

The Statutes of Henry VII.
In Exact Facsimile, From the Very Rare Original, Printed by Caxton in 1489

ISBN/EAN: 9783337250591

Printed in Europe, USA, Canada, Australia, Japan

Cover: Foto ©Thomas Meinert / pixelio.de

More available books at **www.hansebooks.com**

THE STATUTES

OF

HENRY VII.

*IN EXACT FACSIMILE, FROM THE VERY
RARE ORIGINAL, PRINTED BY
CAXTON IN 1489.*

EDITED, WITH NOTES AND INTRODUCTION,

BY

JOHN RAE,

MEMBER OF THE ROYAL INSTITUTION.

LONDON:
JOHN CAMDEN HOTTEN, 74 AND 75, PICCADILLY.
1869.

INTRODUCTION.

———◦⋆◦———

THE following volume of Statutes, comprising those enacted in the first three Parliaments of Henry VII., is a facsimile of the earliest collection of English laws ever printed, and besides containing much information illustrative of the politics, trade, and domestic affairs of England, is further remarkable as being in our native tongue, and not in the Norman-French, which from the time of the Conquest had been employed for such purposes. It is a production of Caxton's press, and probably was one of the last works published by the father of our typography. The third Parliament of Henry VII. met in the year 1489, and Caxton died about 1491 or 1492, the record of his death appearing in the Account Book for that time of the churchwardens of St. Margaret's, Westminster. This book is in the Grenville collection, and within it is a slip of paper, on which appears the following autograph note of Mr. Grenville:

"Statutes of Henry 7, s. a. l. (Caxton).

"A small fragment of this volume was all that had been seen by Ames, or Herbert, or Dibdin till Lord Spencer was enabled to buy the only perfect copy, which was long considered as unique till this year of 1843, in which I purchased this beautiful and perfect copy : a detailed description of it is written by Dibdin for the *Gentleman's Magazine,* 1811, p. 232, being afterwards printed in Bib. Spencer, Vol. IV., p. 344."

Ames (see ed. 1810 by Herbert, with additions by Dibdin) says that Caxton published the Statutes made in the first, second, and third Parliaments of Henry VII., fo., type No. 3.

Lowndes gives amongst the works of Caxton, the Acts 1st, 2nd, and 4th of Henry VII.

Mr. Blades, in his Life and Typography of Caxton, states that only four perfect copies of the present work are known, viz. :

One in the Library of the Inner Temple, another known as Earl Spencer's, a third in the Grenville collection at the British Museum, and a fourth in the Imperial Library of Paris ; adding, however, that a copy is in the possession of A. B. Middleton, Esq., which, he observes, is imperfect, wanting all after signature e, j.

The first of these he describes as in tolerable preservation. In many places it is scribbled upon : is generally soiled ; the margins being in some places stained, and the latter leaves worm-eaten : all the typographical details agree with those of the Grenville copy.

With reference to the copy mentioned by Mr. Blades as being in the French Imperial Library, inquiries having been made of M. Vaschéreau, the Administrator General Director of that establishment, with a view to ascertain the condition of the work, that gentleman states there is no copy of Caxton's work in the Library, and never has been one, but that the Library contains a copy of Pynson's Nova Statuta (1497), a work which is noticed very disparagingly by the Editors of the Statutes of the Realm printed by order of Geo. III., in the year 1817. M. Vaschéreau also remarks that there is no copy of Caxton's work in the Bibliothèque Impériale du Louvre.

It is probable that Mr. Blades trusted to the report of some one less erudite than himself, and who confounded the productions of Caxton with those of another early English printer.

Thus the number of perfect copies is reduced to three ; the Spencer copy, it is to be remarked, differing in some respects from the other two : for example, the chapter in the latter headed, *Felde*, is in the former entitled *Felde in batteyll* : many of the chapters are in a different order of rotation. These discrepancies have been ascertained to exist, from Dibdin's printed statement of the contents, confirmed by the present Librarian at Althorpe. The Spencer copy has likewise some of the leaves stained by the mildew arising from damp, and is moreover slightly wormed. The Grenville copy, the original of our Facsimile, is in very beautiful preservation, and altogether far surpasses the other two copies. Mr. Blade remarks that there are thirty-one lines to a full page ; thirty-two lines, however, occasionally occur in all the copies. There is no place or date, printer's name, or any device impressed upon any of the copies.

Besides the above, it is probable that a few leaves may have been found in some collection, and which enabled Dibdin to give his account of the book, since no perfect copy was known to be then existent.

The period to which these Statutes refers is one of the most interesting in our national history. In the reign of Henry VII., the social state of England received an impetus, which ever since has been exercising a powerfully beneficial influence on the Institutions of the Country, and which has materially conduced to our present prosperity, and advanced civilization. During the greater part of the previous century the land was waste; Agriculture and Commerce were neglected ; while savage rivalry, and discord, fermented by the long wars waged between the rival factions of York and Lancaster, had well nigh depopulated the country ; but when the death of Richard III, and the marriage of Henry, the head of the house of Lancaster, with Elizabeth princess of York, had removed the jealousies, and consolidated the interests of the two families, and when, moreover, many of the turbulent Barons, who, during the time of strife and anarchy had revelled in lawless independence, were reduced by the force of necessity to submission, then the prospect of peace and general amelioration presented itself, which the King earnestly sought to realise. His endeavours were supported by the Commoners, who were clamorously desirous of asserting their rights, and securing their personal liberties against the unbearable inflictions of the Nobles. Henry was well fitted for the task thus undertaken. He was of a calm, deliberate and reserved disposition ; full of energy and industry ; loving order and peace without fearing war ; his capacity was excellent, and, whatever were the motives which guided him in his policy, it is beyond dispute that most of his laws were good, and that he rendered the nation very eminent service. " Certainly," says Bacon, in his striking and masterly life of this prince, " his times for good commonwealth laws did excel, so as he may justly be celebrated for the best lawgiver to this nation after King Edward the First. For his laws (whoso marks them well) are deep and not vulgar : not made upon the spur of a particular occasion for the present, but out of providence for the future, to make the estate of his people still more and more happy, after the manner of the legislators in ancient and heroical times." This brilliant commendation, however, must be taken with some exception. Bacon himself, with his contemporaries generally, entertained very imperfect and erroneous ideas on some points of internal administration and the principles of commerce ; it must also be remembered that the matured laws which now govern commercial transactions were wholly unknown in the fifteenth century. The laws framed by Henry VII, for the direction of the police, were conceived with better judgment than those he enacted for the regulation of commerce : this may be accounted for by the fact that the requirements of the internal administration of Justice lie on the surface, and a simple notion of order and equity will enable the legislator fully to grasp them ; but the principles of commerce are more deeply seated and more complicated : long experience, deep reflection, and a sound discrimination alone can enable a statesman thoroughly to master their intricaces. Moreover, a longer interval is necessary to show the results of laws affecting trade and commerce, and these results often prove quite contrary to the anticipation. Thus it was with Henry's prohibitory laws, limitations, restrictions, and monopolies of trade, many of which were calculated seriously to retard the progress of commerce. It could not however be expected that one, who, in his early days, had been more conversant with war than with commerce, should be wholly in advance of his age on a subject requiring a combination of faculties seldom to be found in the capacities of Monarchs. Monopolies were characteristic of the time, and continued in vogue for more than two centuries after : grants of them formed one of the sources whence the crown drew money as a price of, or by means of which it rewarded or secured an adherent. Monopolies were never more freely created than in the reign of Elizabeth : the Lansdowne MSS. show that they were in daily request, when the great Lord Burleigh administered the affairs of the kingdom : Raleigh held a license to export broad and other cloths, and to vend wines. So far the fashion of the time, and, from the reign of Henry VII., it required more than three centuries of Time's teaching, ere the people could discover that the mutual adoption, by the family of nations, of the principles of freedom in trade, is the most powerful promoter of international prosperity.

Henry VII. assembled his first Parliament within three months after his coronation on Monday, November 7th, 1485 ; his reasons for calling this meeting were fourfold : 1st, To cause the crown to be entailed upon himself and his line (the Act passed for this purpose is not in the present volume ; it is entitled Titulus Regis : but does not appear in any of the early printed collection of Statutes, but is inserted in the Petyt MS. in the Library of the Inner Temple) : 2nd, To have the numerous attainders of his adherents reversed, and to proclaim an amnesty for all acts of hostility committed by them for his benefit : 3rd, To attaint some of the principal leaders of the Yorkist party : 4th, Thereafter to calm and allay the fears of that party by an extensive pardon, well knowing in what danger a King stands from his subjects, when large numbers of them are conscious that their own safety is uncertain. Having thus secured the general peace of the country, Henry directed his attention to the security of his officers, and of all his subjects, particularly the Commoners. Numerous laws were framed for the repression of murder and man-slaughter, crimes of frequent occurrence in consequence of the turbulence of the times ; but his ever constant aim was to lessen the power and influence of the ancient nobility, and to create new families and churchmen ; and as these recently ennobled were naturally more dependent upon him than were the old aristocracy who enjoyed large hereditary possessions, and wielded the influence of ancient names, he rightly judged that the prospect of further favours would render them still more active in his service and obsequious to his demands. In order to carry out his policy of depressing that ancient nobility whose interests so often antagonized with his own, and many of whom were possessed of privileges and jurisdic-tions dangerous to royal authority, the King caused laws to be enacted which tended materially to lessen their power. One of his first Statutes, for this object, was that against the giving of Livery (3 Henry VII., c. 1), and a Session scarcely passed during his reign without the operation of some enactment against engaging retainers, and giving them liveries and badges. This practice, which may appear of little importance to the interests of the State, had at that time grown to be a source of serious embarrassment to the crown. Many enactments relating to it were made even before the time of Henry VII. In the first year of the reign of Henry IV., ch. 17, the giving of liveries was for-bidden except by the King, and even these were not to be worn but in his presence, except in times of war. This enactment was confirmed in the second year of his reign; re-confirmed together with the 1st Statute of Rich. II. c. 7, in the seventh year, and all previous Statutes to the same effect were again ratified in the thirteenth year. By 8th Henry VI., c. 4, Justices of the Peace were directed to proceed against all persons transgressing the laws on this subject. A Livery generally consisted of a hat or hood, a badge, and a suit of clothes. In consequence of the feuds which this custom of giving Liveries engendered, the license to give them became an honour at last granted only to persons of uncommon distinction. The signs and tokens mentioned by the Statute were badges and cognizances; badges were the master's device, crest or arms on a separate piece of cloth, (or, as in the time of Elizabeth, on silver), in the form of a shield, worn on the left sleeve, by domestics and retainers, and even by younger brothers, who wore the badge of the elder; this was generally continued till the time of James I., after which it was only worn by watermen, and servants of persons of distinction. The Royal watermen, when on duty, still wear it. Cognizances were sometimes knots or devices worn in the cap or on the chest; some of the Royal servants wore the King's arms both on the breast and on the back. Reteyndres appear to have been the agreements, verbal, or written, by which the retainers, sometimes called Retinue, (Retynew, vide the Statute entitled *Reteyndour*) were engaged or retained. The possession of Retainers and Liveries led to much abuse; great Lords were in the habit of engaging a number of retainers, who were not maintained as servants, but were trained to warlike exercises. Thus we read that, in the reign of Henry VI., the Earl of Warwick frequently

came to London attended by six hundred men
attired in red jackets, embroidered both on the breast,
and on the back with two ragged staves in saltire
—the Earl's badge. In his house six oxen were often
eaten at breakfast, and every tavern in the neighbourhood
kept open doors : for whoever had any acquaintance in
the house of the Earl, might there have as much roast or
boiled meat as he could prick and carry on a long dagger.

In the reign of Queen Mary some of the great
Lords had two hundred retainers, but Elizabeth would
not permit any person to secure more than one hundred.
Thus numbers of men were maintained in vicious
idleness, which naturally generated a restless martial
spirit, so that they were always ready to assist their
masters in every undertaking, whether lawful or otherwise.
The nobility had long vied with each other in increasing
the number of their retainers, and it required all the energy
and rigour of the King to extirpate the evil. An amusing
anecdote is told of his vigilance in this respect. The Earl
of Oxford, the King's favourite general, in whom he
always placed great and deserved confidence, having
splendidly entertained him at the castle of Heningham,
was desirous of making a parade of his magnificence
at the departure of the royal guest, and ordered all his
retainers, in their liveries, to be drawn up in two lines, that
their appearance might be more splendid and imposing.
" My lord," said the King, " I have heard much of your
hospitality, but the truth far exceeds the report. These
handsome gentlemen and yeomen, whom I see on both
sides of me, are no doubt your menial servants?" The
Earl smiled, but professed that his fortune was too
narrow for such magnificence. " They are most of
them," rejoined he, " my retainers, who are come to

do me service at this time, when they know I am honoured with the presence of your Highness." The King started a little, and replied, "By my faith, my lord, I thank you for your good cheer, but I must not allow my laws to be broken in my sight. My attorney must speak with you." In consequence of this conversation with the attorney, Oxford is said to have paid no less than fifteen thousand marks as a composition for his offence.

It is related by Lloyd, in his *Statesmen and Favorites of England*, that Wolsey kept 500 servants, among whom were 9 or 10 Lords, 15 Knights, and 40 Esquires. Henry Lord Marquis Dorset, father of Lady Jane Grey, says in his depositions, taken by the Protector Somerset against the Lord Admiral, anno 1548, "the admiral devising with me to make me strong in my country, advised me to keep a good house, and asked me what friends I had in my country; to whom I made answer that I had divers servants that were gentlemen, etc." From a passage in Smith's *Berkeley Papers*, it appears that even ladies gave liveries; in an account of the journey of Isobel Marchioness of Berkeley, 8th Henry VIII., to London, there occurs, "Item first, xxx. of her livery;" virtually the husbands of such of these women as were married, must have been retainers of her Ladyship's house; probably such were also the male relatives of the single women.* In the Defence of Coney-catching, 1592, the following passage occurs, "Sirha, although

---

* To establish the fact of the general prevalence of this custom, it may be remarked that on the marriage of Charles Duke of Burgundy, with the Lady Margaret of York, when the bride arrived at the Duke's court at Bruges, our author, Caxton, was one of her retinue. He continued in her service for some time afterwards, and received a yearly fee, together with other advantages.

you have a Livery on your backe, and a cognizaunce to countenaunce you withal, and beare the port of a gentleman, yet I see you are a false knave, etc."

The preamble to the statute concerning the Giving of Liveries furnishes a remarkable picture of the state of the nation at that time : " The kyng our sayd souereyn lord remēbreth how bi vnlawfull mayntenaunces gyuynges of liueres signes & tokens & reteyndres by endêtures promyses othes wrytinges or otherwyse embrasaries of his subgettes vntrue demeanynges of shireffes in makynge of panelles & other vntrue retournes by takynge of money. by iurries. by grete riottes & vnlawfull assemblees. The police & good rule of this reame is almost subdued, and for the nonū punyshynge of thise incōuenyences, and by occasion of the premysses noo thyng, or lityll maye be fonde by enquerry. Wherby the lawes of the lond in execucion maye take lityll effecte to thencres of murdres robberies periuries & vnsuertees of all men leuynge and losses of their londes and goodes, to the grete dyspleysur of Almyghty God." Such a condition of affairs doubtless required great discretionary power in the sovereign, and this Henry VII. fully possessed, for scarcely ever had any king of England been invested with a sway more absolute. In order to eradicate the evils enumerated in the above preamble, the authority of the Star-chamber was established, or rather its powers were enlarged and confirmed by Act of Parliament. Bacon describes this Court as " one of the sagest and noblest institutions of this kingdom." Without by any means fully endorsing this opinion, it must be admitted that it was a kind of jurisdiction which partly suited the rude state of the nation, and, in the words of Hume: "The establishment of the Star-chamber, or the enlargement of its power in the reign of Henry VII., might have been as wise as the abolition of it in that of Charles I."

But the most remarkable law of this whole reign is the Statute entitled " De Finibus," by which the nobility and gentry acquired the power of breaking the ancient entails, and of alienating their estates. This law, joined to the elegance, and luxury which was gradually introduced, served to ruin the great fortunes of the barons, but at the same time increased the wealth and importance of the commons. A previous statute prepared the way for the law, which was enacted against enclosures and " for keeping up the houses of husbandry " (4 Hen. VII. c. 19). Enclosures at that time began to be more numerous, in consequence of which arable land was turned into pastures, which were easily managed by a few herdsmen. Tenancies for years, lives, and at will, such as were held mostly by the yeomanry, were turned into demesnes. This had the effect of diminishing the towns, churches, tithes, &c. What the King felt most acutely was the diminution and decay of the subsidy and taxes; for, as Bacon says : " The more gentlemen, ever the lower books of subsidies." It was not, however, advisable to forbid enclosures, for that would have been obstructing the improvement of the patrimony of the kingdom, nor could tillage be compulsory, as that depended on the nature of the soil. Therefore the King took a course by which he obtained his object in an indirect manner. An ordinance was framed, whereby all farms to which twenty acres of land and upwards were attached, should be maintained for ever, together with a sufficient portion of land to be used with them, and to be held un-severed. This, upon forfeiture, was to be taken by seizure of the land itself by the King

and lords of the fee, with half the profits, till the houses
and lands were restored. By this means, as the houses
were maintained they required tenants, and the
land being attached, it became necessary for that
tenant to be a man of some substance, who would
keep the plough going and support hinds and servants.
Hence arose our vigorous yeomanry, a class between
the gentry and the cottagers or peasants: " men bred
not in a servile and indigent manner, but free and
plentyfull."

The statute against " Giving of Livery.", also
ordained the King's suit for murder to be carried on
within a year and a day, whilst before this time
it did not usually commence till after that period
had elapsed, during which interval the friends of the
murdered person frequently compounded with the murderer, who by this means escaped justice. Numerous
other excellent statutes, for the administration of justice
and the government of the kingdom, were made during
the three parliaments of which the present work treats.
It was made felony to abduct women; the admission
to bail was more strictly regulated; fraudulent transfers
were declared null and void; and many other wise
laws were enacted. One statute is somewhat curious :
by an Act it was declared felony in any servant
of the King to conspire against the life of the
Steward, Treasurer, or Comptroller of the King's household, even though the design was not followed by any
overt act. This law, it was thought, had been pro-
cured by the Lord Chancellor, Archbishop Morton, who,
being of a stern and haughty disposition, and knowing
that he had many mortal enemies at Court, provided it
for his own safety. The real purport of his Act he

tried to disguise by making it general, and communicating the privilege to all other counsellors and peers; yet he did not dare to extend it further than to the King's household, lest the gentlemen and commons should have taken umbrage, and considered their ancient liberty and the clemency of the law invaded if the will in any case of felony should be accounted equal to the deed. Yet the reason which the Act gives, "the destruction of the King and the undoing of the realm," is alike to subjects as to servants in Court. "However," says Bacon, "it seems this sufficed the Lord Chancellor's turn at this time, but yet he lived to need a general law, for that he grew afterwards so odious to the country as he was then to the Court."

As before observed, many of King Henry's statutes relating to commerce and manufacture, and intended to promote their welfare, were merely clogs and obstructions. The great error of the period, and which it occupied ages to eradicate, was the restraint upon industry, in consequence of the jealousy of the corporations and mysteries. Some of these limitations the King enlarged, but not sufficiently so as to admit, that competition and emulation alone can ensure continuous progress. Another great error common to the times was that of fixing the prices of various commodities. Thus, with a view to promote archery, it was enacted that no long bows should be sold at a higher price than 6s. 4d. Prices were also affixed to the charges for cloth: a yard of the best scarlet cloth was not to be dearer than 16s., and a yard of cloth of any other colour not more than 11s. "A *rare* thing to set prices by statute, especially on our home commodities," says Bacon, who admired the wisdom of this Act. But the effect of such laws is often different from that expected by their authors : for as it is impossible to fix a standard of excellence in articles of this kind, so will the effect necessarily be that the articles supplied at the minimum statute price must be of a minimum quality. Again, the idea of restricting the price of produce is futile, for the amount of available material cannot be fixed ; and if its supply be scanty, one of two things must result, either the price of the product will be enhanced, or the manufacture must be abandoned. The preamble to another Act ("Price of Hats and Bonnets," 4 Hen. VII. c. 9) shows the fallacy of this system of trade protection, or rather limitation ; for, being united by the bonds of a craft, mystery, or corporation, the maker could govern the market, and demand his own unreasonable prices. In this manner the hatters and cappers are stated to have been in the habit of selling hats and caps, which cost them no more than sixteen-pence, at prices varying from three to five shillings ; this profit, the King thought, was exorbitant, and he therefore reduced the best hats to the price of 1s. 8d., and the best caps to 2s. 8d. each. Equally useless and vexatious were the laws enacted during this reign, prohibitory of the exportation of money, plate, bullion, and even jewelry. Not only foreign traders, but also merchants from Ireland and the Channel Islands, were compelled to expend the proceeds of their sales in England, upon the native commodities of the realm, which was much like reducing commerce to barter. Such precautions, necessarily, were ineffectual, and only caused more of the prohibited articles to be exported. Severe regulations were also made against taking interest on money, which was designated by the name of Usury, Dry Exchange, and New Chevisance, and is described in the statute as a "damnable bargain," the unavoidable consequence of which would be "the common hurt of this land and the great displeasure of God." By the same sweeping Act, all contracts by which interest was paid for the loan of money were branded as usurious, and even the profits of exchange were prohibited on the grounds of religion and political economy. These illogical views continued to be maintained for more than a century and a half after this period. Even so late as the reign of Charles the First, Justice Rastall described interest or usury as "a gain of anything above the principal or that which was lent, exacted only in consideration of the loane, whether it be corn, meat, apparel, wares, or such like, as money." He then proceeded to impress upon "those who think themselves religious and good Christians" that they cannot with a good conscience take even ten per cent., which the statute then allowed, inasmuch as the Scripture says: "Lend, looking for nothing thereby, whereby it is forbidden to take one penny above the principall." The condemnation of interest for the use of money may be ascribed to the ecclesiastics, who were Judges and Advocates in the Civil Courts, giving rise to the adage *Nullus Clericus nisi Causidicus*, and who imported into their arguments and decisions matter from the Ecclesiastical law unknown alike to the Statute and the Common-law of England. The nobility and the other landowners were willing to acquiesce in the doctrine, believing, as they did, in the supremacy of land, and the Sovereign was equally ready to submit to the popular prejudice, engendered and fostered as it was by the feudal system; yet it is somewhat surprising that a Prince so astute as Henry VII. should not have penetrated this mist of error, since he is said to have accumulated and left no less than £1,800,000, most of it under his own key and keeping at Richmond, where he died. Blackstone remarks that the distinguishing characteristic of this reign was that of amassing treasure in the king's coffers. See Baker's Chronicles. Locke in his *Treatise on Interest* says " my money is apt in trade by the industry of the borrower to produce more than 6 per cent.,(then the legal rate),to the borrower,as well as your land, by the labour of your tenant, is apt to produce more fruits than the rent comes to, and therefore deserves to be paid for, as well as land, by a yearly rent."

Henry VIII., in the 37th year of his reign, limited the interest on loans to ten per cent. per annum ; Edward VI. abrogated this law, and it was enacted that no interests upon land could be received, and if any were taken the principal was forfeited to the crown, with fine and ransom at the king's pleasure ; in the 13th Elizabeth this last act was repealed and that of Henry VIII. revived. By a statute of Queen Elizabeth (13 Eliz. c. 8) it was enacted that he who took even under ten per cent. forfeited the interest so taken. It was only by 21 Jam. c. 17,that interest amounting to ten per cent. was allowed ; "upon like cause," observes an old writer, "that moved Moses to give a bill of divorce to the Israelites, as namely, to avoid a greater mischief and for the hardnesse of their hearts."

The foregoing remarks apply to a few of the more important statutes contained in this collection, some of which have exercised a powerful influence in directing this country to that course of commerce, police, and cultivation in which it has ever since persevered. It was from such infantine attempts that the nation, by constant progression, has happily established "the most perfect and most accurate system of liberty that ever was found compatible with government." Not of less interest are some of the laws made by this Sovereign for the police of the kingdom, and from the preambles to them we become conversant with the condition of the country and the state of the people at the period of their enactment. The statute "Against Hunters," for instance, speaks of strange practices, and describes the "inordinate and unlawful hunting," particularly in Kent and Sussex, by divers persons, who went in great numbers into parks and forests, and there hunted by night and by day, "some with painted faces, some with masks, and otherwise disguised and in manner of war arrayed," shewing at the same time that game-laws were then as unpopular with the Commonalty as they had been in previous, and were in subsequent times. Again, the statute for "Commissions of Sewers" gives a remarkable picture of England, where, in that day, in the counties of Gloucester, Somerset, and elsewhere, "by the increase of waters, divers lands and tenements in great quantity" were flooded and destroyed by inundations. So menacing was this evil that it threatened speedily to accomplish "the decrease and destruction of the livelyhood of the King, of the Church, and of other true liege people of this realm." Many things contributed to this condition of affairs, for during the protracted wars, water-courses had been neglected and become choked, dykes were broken down, and other accidents of the same nature had happened, the natural consequences of depopulation. Such things at least, we see, occurred on the banks of the Thames, where, according to the Statute "for the Mayor

of London," within a few years, by tempests and inundations, numerous issues, breaches, and creeks had become
formed, and overrun pastures, meadows, and the
grounds of divers persons. We obtain a further insight
into the misery caused by civil war, and a vicious social
system, in the remarkable preamble to the statute concerning the Isle of Wight, which, in its sober, formal
official phraseology, gives a most striking picture of the
utter desolation of a portion of the land now remarkable
for its genial climate and generally luxurious aspect.
This, in a great measure was attributable to the increasing
practice of enclosing lands and forming large demesnes.
Against this evil, laws are ineffectual. Unless actuated
by exceptional motives, proprietors will not encourage
excessive populousness. Until the time of the Commonwealth there were numerous laws and edicts against depopulation, as also many Acts against the overcrowding of
London, but it does not appear that these enactments
were ever rigorously enforced. The natural course of
improvement at last provided the remedy.

It may be added that Henry fostered other arts of
peace : he greatly enlarged the Royal house at Green-
wich, built by Humphrey Duke of Gloucester, giving
it the name of Placentia ; he also rebuilt Baynard's
Castle, and the Palace at Sheen, now called Richmond,
where he died; he finished the Savoy, and gave it lands
for the support of 200 poor people ; he erected no less
than six houses for Franciscan Friars ; he also gave to
posterity his beautiful chapel at Westminster, which
building Leland calls the Miracle of the World. The
example of the Monarch was largely followed by his
nobles.

A consideration of these old and well-nigh forgotten

laws is interesting, not only to the historical and anti-quarian student, but also to the general reader.

We enter the Chamber of the Past, and from the shelves take down the record of the times long since gone. A quaint volume, hoary with the dust of ages, is carefully and reverently freed from its thick coating, and its pages opened. Although at first the character of the typography and diction appears strange and uncouth, a little patient pondering reveals to us matter and thought, rich with the lore of antiquity ; the dead seem to live again, and the past comes laden with lessons to the present. From the little volume, time-worn and unpre-tending, start out vivid pictures of the old days ; the troubles that perplexed ; the abuses that clung around the customs of our forefathers ; the incidents that marked their every day life come faithfully before us. We identify ourselves with them, not altogether without a suspicion that much of the abuse then existent is closely analagous to the evil of our own day. Even if we are filled with the complacence arising from the present superiority of knowledge and advanced civilization, we may, nevertheless, with much advantage mark the la-bours of our ancestors, in their efforts to construct laws adapted to the exigencies of the times.

Valuable instruction may be gathered from these old statutes, even though we, in the plenitude of our en-lightenment, may be disposed to question their judgment and deny their efficacy. Grotesque blundering in legis-lation is not altogether confined to the times of Cax-ton, and before we depreciate these ancient laws, we must surrender, and consign many of the darlings of modern law to the region of the impracticable and the absurd.

We do well, then, to read and cherish these old enactments, recognising them as the honest endeavour of the men of the time to combat, and if possible alleviate the abuses then afflicting our brave old land.

"An acquaintance, with the ancient periods of our government," says Hume, "is chiefly *useful* by instructing us to cherish our present constitution, from a comparison or contrast with the condition of those distant times. And it is also *curious*, by shewing us the remote and commonly faint originals of the most finished and most noble institutions, and by instructing us in the great mixture of accident which commonly concurs with a small ingredient of wisdom and foresight in erecting the complicated fabric of the most perfect government."

JOHN RAE.

Chislehurst, Kent,
    June, 1869.

¶ The kynge our souereyn lorde henry the seuenth after the conquest by the grace of god kyng of Englonde & of Fraunce and lorde of Irlonde at his parlyament holden at Westmynster the seuenth daye of Nouembre in the first yere of his reigne/To thonour of god & holy chirche/and for the comen profyte of the royame/Bi thassent of the lordes spirituell & temporell/and the comens in the sayd parliamēt assēbled/and by auctorite of the sayd parlyamente hath comē to be made certein statutes & ordenaunces in maner & fourme folowyng/

¶ Fermedowne

FIrste that where dyuerse of the kynges subgettes hauyng cause of accyon by Fermedowne in the descendre or elles in the remayndre By force of ony taill of and for londes & tenementes ben defrauded & delaied of their said accions. And ofte tymes wythout remedy By cause of feoffemētis made of the same londes and tenementes to persones vnknowen to thentent that the demaūdantes shol de not knowe apenst whom they shall take their accion/It is ordeyned stablysshed & enacted/By the adupce of the lordes spyrituell & temporell and the comens in the sayd parlyament assembled and by auctorite of the same that the demaundant in euery suche caas haue his accion apenst the pernour or pernours of the profytes of the londes or tenementes demaunded Wherof ony persone or persones ben enfeoffed to his or their vse/And the same pernour or pernours named as tenaunt or tenaūtes in the said accion haue the same voucheres/And their lien there vpon eide p per/and all other auantages as the same pernour or pernours shold haue had if they were tenaūtes in dede or as their feoffes shold de haue had if the same accion had be conceyued apēst theim

And yf it fortune ony persone to dyscese soo hauyng feof=
fes to thuse of hym. or of his heires/ the sayd heyre beynge
wythin age/Apenst whom suche accion is brought as per=
nour.thermne the same heire haue his age in the sayd accy=
on conueyd apenste hym/ And all other auautages as yf
his auncestre had deyed ceased of the sayd londes ꝗ tenemen
tes soo in demaude/And also it is ordeyned bi the sayd auc
torite/ that all recouerees as shall be in ony suche accyons
agapne suche pernour or pernours.and their heires and their
sayd feoffes and their heires ꝗ the cofeoffes of the sayd per=
nours ꝗ their heires as though the said pernour or pernours
were tenautes in dede. or feoffes to their vse. or their heires
as is aboue sayd of the free holde of the sayd londes ꝗ tene=
mentis/at ony tyme of the sayd accyon vsed/

¶ Apenste strangers made deynzens to paye custo=
mes/ꝗ c̄

¶ Item where in tyme past dyuerse grautes haue be ma
de)by kynge Edwarde aswell by his lettres patentes as bi
actes of parliament to dyuerse marchautis strāgers borne
oute of this reame to be deynzeyns/Wherby they haue ꝗ re=
ioyce suche fredomes ꝗ libertees as doth deynzeyns borne
wythin this reame.aswell in abatement of theiꝝ custome
Whiche they shold bere yf they were noo deynzeyns as in bi
ynge ꝗ sellyng of theiꝝ marchaundyses.to their grete auap=
le ꝗ lucre/And ofte tymes suffre other strangers not deyn=
szeyns deceptfully to shippe and carie grete and notable sub
staunce of marchaundyse.in their names/by the whiche the
sayd goodes be freed of custome in lyke wyse/as they were
goodes of a deynzen. where of righte they oughte to paye
custome as the goodes of straungers .by the whyche they

be gretly auaunſed in ꝛicheſſe and hauour. And after they
be ſoo enricked foꝛ the mooſt parte / they conueye their ſelfe
wyth their ſayd goodes in to theiꝛ owne countrees. Wherin
they ben naturelly boꝛne/ to the grete enpouerſhyng of this
reame / and to the grete hurte and defꝛaude of the kynges
highnes in payment of his cuſtomes. Wherefore it is en:
acted ſtabliſhed and oꝛdeyned by the aduyſe of the ſayd loꝛ:
des ſpꝛituell and tempoꝛell and comens in the ſayd parlia
mente aſſembled and by auctoꝛite of the ſame/ that ony per
ſone made oꝛ here after to be made depnſzen pay foꝛ his mar
chandiſe like cuſtome a ſubſidye as he ought oꝛ ſholde paye
afoꝛe that he were made depnſzen/ ony lettres patentes oꝛ o:
theꝛ oꝛdenauce by parliamēt oꝛ other wyſe.contꝛary to thys
made.not wythſtondynge.

¶ (Noo protectyon be alowed in ony couꝛt at Calays)

¶ Item the kynge our ſouereyne loꝛde/by thaduyſe of the
loꝛdes ſpꝛituell and tempoꝛell /and at the pꝛayer of the co
mens in the ſaid parliament aſſembled.and by auctoꝛite of
the ſame hath enacted oꝛdeyned and ſtabliſſed/that noo pro
tectyon be here after alowable ne alowed in the courte byfo
re the Mayre. conſtables and feliſhyp of marchauntes /of
the ſtaple at calays/ne in the couꝛte byfoꝛe the lientenaunte
conſtable and feliſhip of marchauntes of the ſame ſtaple
ne in the couꝛte byfore the mayre and his bretherne of the
ſame towne of calays. noꝛ in ony other couꝛte or courtes
wythin the ſame towne. or marches there in ony actyon
ſued / or here after to be ſued by ony of the ſayd marcha
untes.theiꝛ factouꝛs/ſeruauntes or attorney s/ayenſte ony
of the ſayd maꝛchauntes/ their factouꝛs ſeruauntes/ or
attoꝛneys.

¶ Correctyon of prestes for Incontynence.

¶ Item for the more sure and lyke reformacyon of prestes clerkes and religyous men culpable or by theyr demerytes openly noysed of incontynente lyuynge in theyr bodyes contrary to theyr ordre/ It is enacted ordeyned and establysshed by the aduyse and assente of the lordes spirytuell and temporell and comens in the sayd parliamente assembled. and by auctorite of the same. that it be lawfull to all archebysshops ʒ bysshops and other ordynaries hauynge epyscopall iurisdiccion to punysshe and chastice suche preestes clerkes and religyous men beynge wythin the boundes of their Jurisdyccion as shall be commytte afore theym by examynacion/ and other lawfull proeff/ requysite by the lawe of the chirche of aduoutre fornycacyon incest/ or ony other flesshly incontynency/ By commyttynge theym to warde and pryson there to abyde/for suche tyme as shall be thoughte to theyr descressions conuenyent for the qualyte and quantite of their trespasses. And that none of the sayd archebysshops bysshops or other ordynaries a forsayd be therof chargeable of to or vpon ony accyon of false or wrongfull impryson ment/ But that they be vtterly therof dyscharged in ony of the cases aforsayd. by vertue of this acte/

¶ Ayenste Tanners and Cordyners

¶ Item that where Tanners in dyuerse partyes of this reame ben wythin theym selfe the mystere of curryng and blackynge of lether insuffyciently/ And also lether insuffyciently tanned/ and the same lether soo insuffyciently wroughte/ as well in tannynge as in corryynge/ and blackyng

they put to sale in dyuerse fayres and markettes and other
places to grete deceyte and hurte of the kynges liege people
And also where it was ordeyned and stablysshed at the par
liament holden at westmynster the seconde yere of the reygne of kynge Henry the seuenth amonge other/that noo cor
dewener nor none other to his vse sholde ocuppe the mysterie of a tanner whiche he occupyed the mysterie of a cordewe-
ner vnder peyne of forfeyture of euery hyde soo tanned By
hym.or by ony other to his vse.vj. shelinges and viij. pens
And that euery tanner sholde also forfeyte for euery hide
by hym tanned Insuffycyently vj.shelinges viij.pens/as in
the same statute more pleynly appereth / The kynge
our sayd souereyne lorde of his noble grace. by the aduyce &
assente of the lordes spyrituell & temperell. and at the prayer of his comens in this presente parliamente assembled
and by auctoritye of the same parliamente/ in eschuyng of
all suche deceytes hath ordeyned and stablysshed that the sayd
ordenaunce made in the sayd seconde yere of kynge Henry
the seuenth. be and stonde in his full force & strength and
be put in due execucyon in all poyntes And ouer that
By the sayd aduyce and auctorite/hath ordeyned and stablisshed that noo tanner whiles he occupyeth the mystere of a
tanner.nor none other to his vse from the feste of the ascen
sion of our lorde nexte comynge. vse the mystere of coriour/
nor blacke noo lether to be putte to sale/ vnder the peyne of
forfeyture for euery hide by the sayd tanner soo coried vj.she-
linges viij.pens / And that noo corier of lether take vpon
hym/to corie ony hyde of lether/But suche as is a fore suffy-
ciently tanned/vpon peyne to lese for euery hyde soo coryed
iij.shelinges iiij. pens/the one parte of the sayd forfeyture &

officers or mynysters of the sayd late duke/none accion be
maynteneo. ne mayntenable ayenst theym or ony of theym.
wythoute the kynges specyall licence. in that behalfe optey
neo / Prouyded allwaye that this presente acte eptende not
ne in ony wyse be auayllable to ony persone or persones abo
ue specifyed of in or for ony murdre or rape of ony other
than was done the daye of the sayd felde or of ony dyssm
commytted or done by theym or ony of theym in ony wyse.
Prouyded also that this acte eptende not. nor be preiudyci;
all to ony persone or persones whiche had the saufgarde of
the kynge our souereyne lorde / generall or speciall for ony
robberies trespasses/ or ony other Iniuries don or comptted
to theym or ony of theym after the saufgarde made/ Under
his pryue seale or sygnet or other warraunt suffycient pro;
uyded allway p this acte ne none other. in this present parli
amete made or to be made be not hurtefull ne preiudyciatte
Unto Elizabeth Wyndesore wedowe. late wyfe of Thomas
Wyndesore esquyer Edwarde Cheseman and sir John Co;
ket prest execuiours of the testament of the sayd Thomas
Wyndesore/ of or for ony robberi e trespasse or other offence
don Unto the sayd Thomas in his lyffe; But that the sayd
Elizabeth Edwarde and John Coket maye haue and pur;
sue actyon or actions ayenst all maner persone or persones
ioyntly and seueratty for the sayd robberyes trespasses and
offences/ And eck of theym by whatsomeuer name or na;
mes the sayd Thomas Wyndesore the sayd Elizabeth Ed;
warde Cheseman and John Coket was or be named.
This acte or ony other acte in this present parliament ma
de or to be made Notwythstandynge .

⸿ Item for as mocke as a fore. this tyme dyuerſe ordena
unces and ſtatutes haue be made in dyuerſe parliamentes
holden in this reame for the punycyon of inordynate and
vnlawfull huntynges/in foreſt parkes/ and in warrenes
wythin the ſayd reame. Whiche ſtatutes & ordeynaunces not
wythſtodynge dyuerſe perſones in grete nombre. ſome with
peynted faces/ſome wyth vyſours/and otherwyſe dyſgyſed
to thentent they ſholde not be knowen ryotouſly and in ma
ner of werre. arrayed haue often tymes in late dayes hun
ted as well by nyghte as by daye in dyuerſe foreſtes par;
kes and warrennes in dyuerſe places of this reame/ And
in eſpecyall in the countye of kente ſurrey and ſuſſex. by co
lour wherof haue enſued in tymes paſt grete and haynous
rebellyons inſurreccyons Riottes robberies murders and
other inconuenyences. to the preuocacyon and enſample of
ryottous and euyll dyſpoſed perſones of this reame/in ſu;
che wyſe to offende. Whiche offenſes were not be duely pu;
nyſſed afore this tyme accordynge to the ſayd ſtatutes orde
naunces & lawes of this ſayd rea.nc. by cauſe the ſayd mif
doers by reaſon of their ſayd paynted faces/ viſours and o;
ther dyſgyſynges were not be knowen   The kynge
our ſayd ſouereyne lorde of his noble and habūdance grace
in conſideracyon of the premyſſes/ by the aduyſe and aſſent
of the lordes ſpyrituell and temporell at the ſupplycacyon
of the comens in the ſayd parliamēt aſſembled and by auc
toryte of the ſame/that at euery ſuche tyme as informacyon
ſhall be made of ony ſuche vnlawfull huntynges by nyght
or wyth paynted faces here after to be done. to ony of the

kynges Councell·or to ony of the Justyces of the kynges
peas/ of the countee where ony suche huntynges shalle be
had of ony persone to be suspect therof/That than it be law
full to ony of the same counsell or Justyces of peas/ to
whome suche enformacyon shall be made/. to make a warra
ūte to the Shyrref of suche countye. or to ony constable. bay
le/or other offycer wythin the same Countye. to take and ar
reste the same persone or persones/of whom suche enforma
cion shall be made. And to haue hym or theym a fore the
maker of the sayd warraunte/ or ony other of the kynges
sayd counsell or Justyces of his peas of the same countye
And that the sayd counsellour or Justyce of peas/ afore
whom suche persone or persones shall be broughte/by his dis
crecyon haue power to examyn hym or theym/soo brought
afore the sayd counsellour or iustyces. of the sayd huntyng
and of the sayd doers in that behalfe. And yf the same per
sone wylfully concele the sayd hutinges/or ony persone with
hym defectyue therin/that thenne the same concelement be a
penst euery suche persone soo concelyng. felonye. And the sa
me felony to be enquyred of. and determyned as other felo
nyes wythin this reame haue bsed to be/And yf he thenne
confesse the trouth/and all that he shall be examyned of and
knoweth in that behalfe / that thenne the same offences of
huntynges by hym done be as apenst the kynge our soue
ry lorde but trespasse fynably by reason of the same confessi
on at the nexte generall sessions of the peas. to be holden in
the same coūtye by the kyngis iustyce of the same sessyons
there to be sessed/ And yf ony rescusse or disobeysaunce be
made to ony persone. hauynge auctoryte to do execu
cyon or iustyce by ony suche warrante by ony persone

the whiche soo sholde be arrested/ Soo that execucion of the
same warzant therby be not had that thenne the same rescu
se and disobepsaunce be felony enquyrable/ and determyna=
ble as is a fore sayd/ And ouer this it is enacted and sta
blysshed by the sayd auctorite . that yf ony persone or perso=
nes here after be commytted of ony suche huntynges wyth
peynted faces bysours or otherwyse dysguysed to thentent
they sholde not be knowen. or of vnlawfull huntynge in ti
me of nyghte .that thenne the same persone or persones soo
commytted haue like punycion as be or they sholde haue/ yf be
or they were competed of felony/

¶ For reperacyons of the Nauee.

¶ Item in the sayd parliament/ it was called to remem=
braunce of the grete mynysshynge and decaye/ that hath be
now of late tyme of the nauye wythin this reame of Eng
londe. and Idlenesse of the maryners wythin the same. Bi the
whiche this noble reame. within short processe of tyme wyth
oute reformacion be had therin. shall not be of habylite and
power to deffende it selfe. Wherefore at the prayer of the sa
yd compns / the kynge our soueryne lorde by the aduyse
of the lordes sprytuell and temprell in this sayd present
parliamente assembled. and by auctorite of the same/ It is
enacted ordeyned and establisshed/that noo maner of persone
of what degree or condycion that he be of. bye nor selle wyth
in this sayd reame/ Irlonde. wales calays/ or the marches
therof. or Berwyk. from the fest of Myghelmas next now
compng. ony maner wynes of the growynge of the duchie
of Guyen or of Gascoygne/ But suche wynes as shalle
be auentured and broughte in an Englisshe / Iryshe or
Walsshe mannys hyppe or shyppes/   And
that the maryners of the same englisshe Irisshe or walsshe

men fyxe the moxe parte / Or men of calays or of the mar=
ches of the same. and that Vpon peyne of forfeiture. of the
same Vvynes soo boughte or solde contrary to this acte the
oon halfe of that forfeiture to be to the kynge our souereyn
lorde. and that other halfe to the fynder of that forfeiture /
This acte & ordenaũce to endure VptVviþ this & the begyn=
nynge of the next parliamēt. Sauyng alVvaye to the kyng
his prerogatyue.

⸿ Item that Vvhere in the parliamēt late holden at Vvestmyn
ster the xx. day of Januarij the xij yere of kyng EdVvarde
the fourth / It Vvas enacted ordeyned & stablysshed by auctory
te of the sayd late parliamēt Vpon many & grete considȝacy
ons and lamētable compleyntes conteyned in the same acte
that noo marchaũt stranger nor other after the fest of Es=
ter than next comyng sholde brynge in to this reame of En
gelonde to be solde ony corses gyrdles rybandes laces calle
sylke or coleyn silke / throVven or Vvroughte Vpon peyn of for
feiture therof / or of the Value therof / in Vvhos handes they
shall be founde / the oon halfe of the sayd forfeiture. to be Vnto
the kyng our souereyn lorde and that other halfe / to be Vnto
hym or theym of his subgettis the Vvhiche shall seas e the sa
me. or sue for the same By accyon of det By Vvritte at comen
laVve / by Bylle or pleynt after the custume of the cyte or toVv
ne Vvhere it shall happen hereafter ony suche forfepture to
falle or be. And that the deffendaũt in ony suche accyon be
not amytted to Vvage or doo his laVve. Nor that ony protec=
cion nor essoyne in the serupce of the kynge for ony suche de
fendaunt be aloVved. The sayd acte to endure for iij. yeres
than nexte ensuynge the sayd feste. The Vvhiche acte after=
Vvarde in the parliamēt holden by Richarde the thirde late in

dx and not in right kynge of Englonde was graunted ꝛ
oꝛdeyned to be ꝑ ſtonde good auaillable ꝛ effectuell Bnto the
ende of the ſayd iiij peres and from thende of the ſame iiij.
peres Bnto thende ꝛ terme of p. peres than nexte enſuynge
The whiche ſayd iiij peres contepned in the ſaid fiꝛſt acte/
ſhal fynyſſe ꝛ eyſpire/at the feſt of eſterne/the whiche ſhall
be in the pere of ouꝛ loꝛde god.M. CCCC.lppp8ij. The
kynge ouꝛ ſayd ſouereyn loꝛde that now is By auctoritè of
this his a foreſaid parlemēt hath oꝛdeyned that the ſayd ac
te ꝛ oꝛdenaūce/as foꝛ the hole bꝛaūch of the ſayd acte ꝛ oꝛde
naunce as feꝛ as toucheth or concerneth theſe prempſſes be
ꝛ ſtonde auaillable ꝛ effectuell Bnto thende of the ſayd iiij.
peres/ And from thende of the ſame iiij.peres/ Bnto thende
ꝛ terme of pp. peres than nexte enſupng/ Notwythſtodpn
ge ony acte oꝛdynaunce graunt or proupſo in this preſente
parlement made or to be made/to ony marchaūt ſtꝛanger or
other/

Revocacion of kyng Ricbardis acte apenſt Italiens/
¶ Itē the kyng ouꝛ ſayd ſouereyne loꝛde Bnderſtondpng
By a ſupplyeacion put Bnto his highnes in this his ſayd
paꝛliament By the maꝛchauntes of Italpe reſidente in this
his ſayd reame of Englonde.that where By an acte of parle
mēte made in the parliament of Richarde late pꝛetendpnge
hym to be kynge of Englonde the thiꝛde holden at weſtmyn
ſter the fiꝛſt pere of his reigne/it was oꝛdeyned ꝛ proupded
that all marchaūtes of the nacpon of Italie a fore reherſed
not made denizenis.Whiche than had or ſhold haue wythin
this reame wares ꝛ maꝛchandiſes bꝛoughte from beponde
the ſee and Bpfore the feſt of Eſter than nexte eſupng ſhold
haue/ſhold do ſelle oꝛ baꝛtre theym in groſe/and not Bp reta
plle to the kyngis ſubgettis afore the fiꝛſte daye of Maye

that thēne sholœ be in the pere of our lorœ god M. CCCC
lxxxv./And the money compnge of the sale byfore the sayd
first daye wypthin the same porte or portes where they arry
ued/ enploye vpon the cōmodytees & march andises of this
reame/their resonable costes & eypēses allwaye excepte and
œducted vpon pyne of forfeiture of the value aswell of al
the sayd wares & marchaudises kepte & not solœ a fore the
sayd firste daye or otherwpse solœ than is a bove sayd/ and
of soo mocke money as sholœ be made ouer by exchauge con
trary to the sayd acte / And that all the sayd marchauntes
of Italy/the which after the sayd feste of Ester brought or
ny marchandyses or wares in to this reame to be solœ shol
œ selle or bartre the same wares & marchandyses in grose
and not by retayle vnto the kynges subgettes vpon pyne
of forfeiture of the value of the same wares & marchaudy
ses otherwpse solœ/ And that the sayd marchauntes their
sayd wares & marchaudises which they sholœ bryng after
the sayd fest of Ester shold œo bartre or selle the same with
in viij monethes nexte after their first arriual in to this re
ame in fourme a foresaid/and the money compng of or bi p
sayd sales or bartrynges of theim and eueri of theim enploy
and ther wpth bye the cōmoditees or marchaudises of thps
reame of englonœ wypthin the sayd viij monethes in the sa
me porte or portes where they shold first arryue/their resona
ble costes & expenses allwaye excepte & œducted · And that
they sholœ in noo wpse make ony sucke money ouer by ex
chaunge / And the sayd marchautes/ thepr sayd wares &
marchandyses remaynynge vnsolœ/after thenœ of the say
œ viij. monethes in no wpse sholœ selle nor bartre wypthin
the sayd reame. But sholœ carye & conueye theym oute of the
same reame. wypthin ij. monethes than nexte folowynge

after the sayd .viij. monethes yf wynde and weder wyll se
ue it/ And els as soone as wynde & weder wolde serue them
after the sayd two monethes vpon peyne of forfeyture as
well of as moche money as sholde be made out of this said tr
aine by exchauge as of the sayd wares & marchadises soo
solde or bartred after thende of the sayd viij monethes not
carried ne coueyed out of this sayd reame/in fourme afore
sayd or the value therof the forfeitures penalte & losse of al
the premysses to renne & be vpon the said marchautes of J
talie doyng contrarie to this acte/ And also that noo straū
ger of what coūtrey so euer he were sholde oost or take to so
iourne woith him wythin this reame of Englond ony mar
chaute straūger not beyng of the same nacion that he sholde
be of/ vpon peyne to forfeyte & lose at euery tyme that he soo
dyde. xl li. And that noo marchaunte straunger sholde be at
ooste ne soiourne wyth ony other marchaut stranger not be
yng of his nacyon/or coūtrey wythin the sayd reame vpon
peyne of .xl li. And that noo straūger sholde bie ony wolle
the whiche sholde be sent or passe thrugh the streyttes of Mar
rok. by galayes or carekes or shyppes or other vesselles sor
ted clakked or barbed/nor ony wolle wherof lockes or re
fuse sholde be made/but that the same wolle/sholde be as it we
re shorne & clene woude/ wythout ony shortyng barbynge or
clakkyng or lokkes or refuse therof to be made. as it is afore
sayd. vpon peyne of forfeiture of the same woll/and the dou
ble value therof/as by the same acte more playnly may ap
pere. Also that the sayd marchautes of Jtaly sholde haue &
coueye their wolle wollencloth/and all other their marchan
dyses ouer the streittes of marrok. vpon peyne of forfeiture
of the same/as by the same acte playnly apereth/ The kyn
ge our sayd souereyne lorde by thadyce of the lordes spiri<!--
-->

tuell and temporell/and comens in this present parliamen
te assembled. and by auctorite of the same/hath ordeyned sta
blisshed and doo to be enacted that the aboue sayd forseitures
penaltees seisours & actions comprised in the sayd actes &
euerich of hem. be reuoked voide annulled & of noo streng;
the agaynst all maner personnes/excepte & reserued oonly to
the kyng/to be at libertye/ to haue & enioye all maner seiso;
urs forseites & penaltees in the sayd actes specifyed. And
that it be liefull to the kyng to graute to his sayd besecheres
his lettres of saufcondupt & lettres patentes surely to be en
ioyed . accordyng to the tenours therof/ the aboue sayd acte
& actes notwithstondyng/in as ample wyse as though thei
had neuer be had nor made/

¶ The seconde parliament holden the thirde yere of kyng
Henry the vij.

The kynge our soueroyne lorde Henry by the grace
of god kynge of Englonde & of Fraunce & lord of
Irlonde the vij. at his parliamente holden at West;
mynst the ix. day of Nouembre in the thirde yere of his no;
ble reigne/To the worship of god & holy chirche/and for the
comen wele of this his reame / by thaduys & assente of the
lordes spirituell & temperell & the comens in the sayd parlia
ment assembled. and by auctorite of the same parliamente
hath ordeyned & establisshed certeyn statutes & ordenauces in
maner & fourme as here after ensueth/
　　　　　　¶ Yeuynge of lyuerey/& c.
¶ Fyrst the kyng our sayd soueroyn lord/remembreth how bi

Bnlalbfull mayntenaunces gyuynges of liueres signes ꝙ
tokens ꝙ retoynores By endetures prompses othes Woytin
ges or otherwyse/embiasaries of his subgettes Bn true de:
meanynges of shireffes in makynge of panelles ꝙ other
Bntrue retournes By takynge of money.By iurries.By grete
riottes ꝙ Bnlawfall assembles . The police ꝙ good rule of
this reame is aimost subdued/and for the nonu punyshyn
ge of thise ineouenpences/ and By occasion of the premps:
ses noo 'Byng/or lityll maye be fonde By enquerry. Wherby
the lawes of the lond in execucion maye tasie lityll effecte
to thencres of mardres robberies periuries ꝙ Bnsuerttes of
all men kuynge and losses of their londes ꝙ goodes/ to the
grete opsplepsur of almyghty god / Therfore it is ordeyned
for reformacyon of the prempsses By auctorite of the sayd
parliament/That the cBauceller ꝙ tresorer of Englonde for
the tyme beyng ꝙ keper of the kyngis priue seale.or ij.of the
ym/callyng to hym a byshop ꝙ a temperall lord of the kyn:
gis moost honorable couseyll. and the ij. chief iustices of ỿ
kyngis Bencke ꝙ comen place/for the tyme beyng.or other ij.
iustices in their absence/ Bpon bylle or informacion put to
the sayd chauceller for the kyng.or ony other agayn ony per
sone/for ony mysehaupng afore rehersed. haue auctorite to
calle Byfore theym By thii or priue seale.the sayd mysdoers
And theym ꝙ other By their descrecions By whom /the two:
uth may be knowen to examyn and sucke as they fynde ther
in defectpf/to punysshe theym after their demerites/after the
fourme ꝙ effect of statutes therof made/in like maner ꝙ so
urme as they shold and ought to be punyshed yf they were
therof conuycte. after the due ordre of the lawe/And ouer
that it is ordeyned By the auctoryte aforsayd/that the Justy
ces of the peas of euery shyre of this reame / for the tyme

beyng maye doo take By their dyscrecyon an enqueft Wherof
eueri man fhall haue londes ҁ tenementis to the yerely Ba
luze of ҁl. fheiinges at the leeft to enquere/of the concelemē
tis of other enqueftes taken afore thepm.and afore other of
fuche mateis ҁ offences as ar to be enquerwd/and prefented
afore Juftyces of peas/ Wherof complynte fhall be mad/By
Byllẽ oz Bylles/aſwell Wythin frauchiſe as Without/And
yf ony fuche concelement be foūd of ony enqueſt as is afo:
re rehersed/had or made Wythin the yere/after the fame conce
lement/eueri perfone of the fame enqueſt to be amerced for ẏ
fame concelementis By dyfcrecyon of the fame Juftices of
the peas/the fayd ameiciamentes to be feffed in plynte feſſi:
ons   Jtem the kyng remembreth how murdres ҁ fleyng
of his fubgettis daily encreſe in this lond/thoccaſion Wher
of be dpuerſe/one that noo men in townes Where fuche mui
dres happe to fall and be won/Wylſe not attacke the mui:
drer Where the lawe of the lond is that if ony man be fleyn
in the daye/and the felon not taken/the townſhyp Where the
deth oz murdre is won fhall be amerced.And if ony man be
Wouded in prill of deth.the partie that foo Woūdeth fhold be
arreſt ҁ put in fuertie/tyll parfyght knowlege be had Whe:
der he foo hurte fhold liue oz deye/And the coroner Bpon the
Sieue/of the body.ҁc.fhold inquire of hym oz thepm that
had won that deth oz murdre of their abettouis ҁ conſento:
urs/And who were prefente Whan the deth oz murder was
won Whether man oz woman/ And the names of thepm
that were prefente/and foo founde to enrolle and certifye/
Whiche lawe By neclicence is difufed . and therby grete
boldeneffe is gyuen to fleers and murdrers.And ouer this
it is Bfed that Wythin the yere ҁ daye after ony deth oz mur
dre hade and won/the felon fhold not be determyned at the

kyngis sute. fox sauyng of the partie sute/Wherein the par⸗
tie is oftymes slowe/And also agreed wyth. and by then⸗
ce of the pere. all is forgoten / Whiche is a nother occasyon
of murder/And also he that wylle sue ony appell. moste sue
in propre persone Whiche sute is longe/ and costely. that it
maketh the partie appellant wery to sue/ For reformacyon
of the premysses.   The kyng our souereyne lorde by thas⸗
sent of the lordis spirytuell & temporell. and the comens in
the sayd parliament assembled/and by auctorite of the same
wylle that euery coroner exercise & do his offyce. accordyng
to the lawe. as is afore rehersed/ And that yf ony man be
slayn or murdred . and therof the sleers murderers abbetto⸗
urs mayntenours & consortours of the same be endyted. that
the same sleers & murderers/and all other ascessories of the
same/be arrayned and determyned of the same felonye and
murder at ony tyme at kyngis sute/ Wythin the pere. after the
same felonye & murder don/and not tary. the pere & day/for
ony appele to be taken for the same felony or murder. And
yf it happen ony persone named as pryncypall or ascessorye
be acquyted of ony suche murder/at the kyngis sute. Wyth
in the pere & daye/that thenne the same Justyces afore who⸗
me he is acquyted shall not suffre hym to goo at large/ But
eyther to remytte hym ayen to pryson/or elles to lete hym to
bayle after theyr dyscrecyon tyll the pere and daye be passed
And yf it fortune that the same felons or murderers & ac⸗
cersories soo arrayned. or ony of theym to be acquyte or the
pryncypall of the sayd felonye/or ony of theym to be attern⸗
ted/the wyffe or nexte heyre/to hym soo slayne as shall re⸗
quyre maye take and haue theyr appele of the same deth &
murdre wythin the pere/and daye after the same felonye &
murder done ayenste the sayd persones soo arrayned and
                                                                    . B   iij

acquyte. And all other their accefſories or ayenſt the accef
ſories of the ſayd pryncipall/or ony of them ſoo atteynted
or ayenſt the ſayd pryncyppallis ſoo atteynted / yf they ben
on lyue. And the benefyte of his clergye. therof before not
had. And that the appelaunte haue ſuche and like auaun=
tage as yf the ſayd acquytalle or atteyndre notwythſton=
dyng. And ouer that the wyfe or heyre of the ſayd perſon
ſoo ſlayne or murdred/as caſe ſhall requyre maye comence
theyr appell in propre perſone/at ony tyme wythin the ye=
re. after the ſayd felony won before the ſhiriff and corners
of the countie where the ſayd felonye/and murder was won
or before the kynge in his benche or Juſtyces of Gayoll de
liuerer/And the appellaunte in ony appelles of murder or
deth of man where Batell by the cours of the comen lawe/li
eth not make theyr attourneys. and appere by the ſame/ in
the ſayd appelles/after they be commenſed to the ende of the
ſute and execucyon of the ſame/And yf ony perſone be ſlai
ne or murdred in the daye. And the murderer eſcape vnta=
ken/that the townſhyp where the ſayd ded is ſoo won be a=
merced for the ſayd eſcape/ And that the corner haue auc=
torytee to inquyre therof vpon the biewe of the body ded.
And alſo iuſtyces of peas haue power to inquyre of ſuche
eſcapes/and that to certifye afore the kynge in his benche/
And that after the felonye founde/the corners deluer the
pr Inqupſicyons afore the iuſtyces of the nexte gayoll deli=
uerer in the ſhyre where inqupſicyon is taken the ſame iuſ
tyces to procede agaynſte ſuche murderers yf they ben in the
gayole. And elles the ſame Juſtyces to put the ſayd Inquy
ſicyons afore the kynge in his benche/ And for as moche
as corners had not nor ought ony thynge to haue by the
the lawe. for theyr offyce doyng / Whiche ofte tymes hathe

ken the occasion that cozoners haue ken rempsse/ in woyng
their offyce   Jt is ordeyned that a cozoner haue for his
fee.Vpon euery inquisicyon taken Vpon the Vyeue of the bo
dy slayne.xiij.skelinges iiij.pens of the goodis and catal=
les of hym/that is the sleer and murderer yf he haue ony go
des/And yf he haue noo goodes/ thenne the cozoner to ha=
ue for his sayd fee/of suche amercyamentes as shall fortu
ne ony townshyp to be amersed for escape of suche murdre.
as is aforesayd/And yf ony cozoner be rempsse and make
not his inqupsicyons Vpon the Vyeue of the body ded/z cer
tifye it not accozdynge as is afore ordeyned . that the cozo=
ner for euery defawte forfeyte to the kynge.C.skelinges
And also it is ordeyned by the same auctorite / that euery
Justice of peas Wythin this reame/ that shall take ony re=
conysaunce for the keppynge of the peas that the same Justi
ces do certifye/ sende or brynge the same reconysaunce atte
the nexte sessions of peas / Where he is or haue ken Justyce/
that the partye soo bounde.may be called And yf the partye
make defawte.the same defawte than there to be recorded
And the same reconysaunce Wyth the recorde of the defaw
te be sente and certefyed in to the Chauncerie/ oz afore the
kynge in his bencke/or in to the kynges eschequer /

⁋ Takynge of maydens/Wedowes z Wyues
agenste theyr Wylle is made felonye /

⁋ Item Where Wymmen as Well maydens as Wedowes
and Wyues/hauynge substaunces /some in goodes mouable
and some in londes and tenementes / and some beynge hey=
res apparaunt Bnto their auncestours/ for the lucour of su
che substaunces ken often tymes taken.by mysdoers contrari
to theyr Wylle/And after marved to suche mysdoers oz to

other By theyr assente. or desopted to the grete dysplysur of
god. and contrarie to the kynges lawes/and dispergement
of the sayd wymmen. and bitter heupnesse & dyscomforte of
their frendes. and to the euyll ensample of all other.   It
is therfore ordepned establisshed & enacted By our sayd soue=
reyne lorde the kynge By thassente of the lordes spirytuell &
temporell/and the comens in the sayd parliamente assem=
bled. and By auctorite of the same/that what persone or per=
sones fromhensforth that taketh ony woman so apenst hyr
wylle/Bnlawfully.that is to sape.Mayde wydowe or wyfe
that suche takynge procurynge and abbettynge to the same
And also recepuynge wylyngly the same woman soo ta=
ken apenste her wylle/ and knowynge the same. be felonye /
And that suche mysdoers takers & procuratours to the sa=
me . and recettours knowynge the sayd offence in fourme
aforsayd be hensforth reputed and iudged as pryncppall fe=
lons.   Prouyded alwaye that this acte extende not to o=
ny persone/takynge ony woman onely clamyng her as his
warde or bonde woman/

¶ Letyng to Bayle of psones arrested for light suspeccyon
¶ Item Where in the parliamente late holden at westmyn=
ster the firste pere of Picharde late in dede/ and not in ryghte
kynge of Englonde the thirde/ It was ordepned and enac=
ted amonges other dyuerse actes/ that euery Justyce of the
peas in euery shyre cyte or towne shold haue auctorite and
power by his or their dyscresyon to lete prisoners and per=
sones arrested for lighte suspectyon of felonye in Baylle or
maynprice.By colour wherof.afterwarde dyuerse persones su
che as were not maynpreuable were often tymes letten to
Baylle & maynpryse By iustyces of peas apenst the due four
me of the law/wherby many felons escaped to the grete dis=
plesur of the kyng/and anoyaunce of his liege peple. wher

fore the kyng our said souerayn lord consideryng it by thad
uyse & assent of the lordes spirituell & temporel & the comēs
in the said parliament assembled. and by auctorite of the sa
me·hath ordeyned establisshed & enacted/that the iustyces of
the peas in euery shire | cyte & towne/or two of thepm at þ
leest wherof one be/of the quorū/. haue auctorite & power to
lete ony suche prysoners or persones maynpernable by the
lawe. that ben imprysoned wythin their seuerall coūties ci
te or towne to baylle or maynprise . Bnto their neyte gene
rall sessions/or bnto the next gaiolle deliuerer of the same
gaiolles in eueri shire cite or towne/ aswell wythin frau
chies as wythout. where ony suche gaiolles ben· or bere af
ter shall be/And that the sayd iustyces of the peas or one
of thepm/soo takyng ony suche bayll or maynpryse/ doo cer
tifie the same/at their neyte generall sessions of the peas/or
the next generall gailes deliuerāce of ony suche gaile with
in eurry suche coūtie cite or towne next folowyng.after ony
suche bayll or mainprise soo taken bpon peyn to forfeyt bn
to the kyng/for euery defaute ther bpon recorded x. li. And
ouer that it is enacted by the same auctorite/that eueri shir
ref bayllif of frauchise·and euery other persone/hauyng au
torite/or power of kepyng of gaylis or of prisoners for fe
lonye/in liKe maner & fourme doo certifye the names of e
ueri suche prisoner in their keping & of euery prisoner to the
pm comptted for ony suche cause/at the neyte generall gay
le deliuerer in euery coūtie or frauchies where ony suche goi
le or gayles ben or berafter shall be/there to be calendred by
fore the iustices of the deliuerance of the same gayle. wherby
they may aswell for the kyng as for þ partie procede to ma
Ke deliuerance of suche prisoners acordyng to the law bpon
peyne to forfeyte bnto the kyn ge for euery defawte therw

recorded an hundred stelinges/ And that the forsayd acte
peupnge auctoryte and power in the premysses to ony oon
Justice of the peas by hym selfe . be in that behalfe . Vtterly
voyde.and of none effecte by auctoryte of this presente par
liamente/

 Dedes of gyftes of goodes to thuse of the maker
of suche gyfte be voyde/

 Item that where often tymes dedes of gyftes of goodes
 catalles/ben made to thentent to defraude their creditours
of their duties/And that persone or persones that maketh
the sayd dede of gyfte goeth to seyntuarie / or other places
prpupleged/and ocuppeth liueth wyth the sayd goodes
catalles / their credytours beyng vnpayed . It is ordeyned
enacted stablisshed by thassent of the lordes spirituell tem
porell/and at the requeste of the comens in the sayd parlia:
ment assembled ane by auctoryte of the same/that all dedes
of gyfte/of goodes catalles made or to be made of trust. to
thuse of that persone or persones/that made the same dede of
gyfte be voyde.and of none effecte.

 Drye exchaunge

 Item for asmoche as importable domages losse enpo
uersshing of this reame.is had bi dampnable bargeyns gro
wed in vsurie coloured by the name of newe cheupsance co
trary to the lawe of naturell Justyce. to the comen hurte of
this londe.and to the grete displeasur of god/Our sayd so:
uereyn lord the kyng for the reformacyon therof of all co
rupt vnlefull bargeyns. By thassent of the lordis spirituel
 temporell and the comens in his sayd parliamente assem:
bled/and by auctoryte of the same hath ordeyned enacted
that if herafter ony bargein couenaut by byeng of ony obli:
gacion/bille or by ony pleges put for suerte. or bi bylle/or o
ther wyse/

By the name of dꝛye eſchaunge oꝛ otherwyſe woꝛerby ony
certeyn ſome ſhall be loſte by ony couuenaunte oꝛ pꝛomeſſe
Bytwyx ony perſone oꝛ perſones by theymſelf / oꝛ ony other
to their knowlecke wythin this reame/oꝛ yf ony baꝛgein oꝛ
loue/woꝛerby ony of the partie ſholde leſe. oꝛ paye for ony ſo
me certeyn.that is to ſaye / for hauyng a hundꝛed pounde in
money/ oꝛ marchandyſe oꝛ otherwyſe/And therfoꝛe to pay
oꝛ fynde ſuertie to paye ſix ſcoꝛe pounde. oꝛ moꝛe oꝛ leſſe/ in a
for ony moꝛe oꝛ leſſe ſome after ony maner rate. that all ſu
che baꝛgaynns couenauntes pꝛompſe a ſuertyes therfoꝛe
made/and all thyng therof dependyng/ be vtterly voyde and
of none effecte/ And ouer this it is oꝛdeyned by the ſame auctorite/that yf ony marchandyſes obligacyons byl/.
les oꝛ plate be pꝛompſed to be delivered vpon ſuche corrupte
baꝛgens and neuer delivered oꝛ delivered and had agayn
to hym that oughte ſuche marchaundyſes/obligacions byl
les oꝛ plate/oꝛ knoweth by ony other man by aſſent aggre
mente/oꝛ knowlecke in ony maner fourme ! of hym oꝛ his
factouꝛ oꝛ bꝛoker that ſuche marchaundyſes oughte.and oꝛ
pꝛyuee to ſuche baꝛgeynns/that all ſuche baꝛgeyns couenau
tes pꝛompſes/and all ſuerties therfoꝛe made/be vtterly voy
de/And ſeller owner baꝛgeyner oꝛ pꝛompſer of ſuche corup
te baꝛgayns oꝛ goodes leaſe for ony ſuche baꝛgeyn made/bi
hym oꝛ his factour C.li. And whoſoeuer wyll ſue therfo-
re/ to haue an action of dette.in whiche the partye ſhall not
wage his lawe.the kynge to haue the one half/and he that
wylle ſue the other half. And foꝛ as moche as theſe corrupte baꝛgeyns ben mooſt vſuelly had wythin cytees
a boꝛughs /hauynge auctorite to trye alle maters a cauſes
growen a had wythin the ſame cities a bꝛughs.and if ony
ſuche defautes ſholo there be tryed/periury by likelynes therby

ſholde growbe/and litpll of the prempſſes to be founde/Ther
fore it is ordepned by the ſapd auctorpte that aſwell the cha
unceller of Englonde for the tpme kepng haue auctorite ꝫ
powber to epampn almaner corrupte bargepns prompſes to
nes or ſales growben ꝫ had of onp of the prempſſes/And
therupon by his exampnacion to here and determpne the ſa:
me/and to gpue like iugemente and make like erecucpon
therof as the mater wbere tried ꝫ founde/ at the parties ſute/
in onp ſuche action of dette by the cours of the compn lawe
as the iuſtpces of the peas of onp ſhpre nept adiopnpng to
onp cite or burgh wbere ſuche defautes be·of onp of the pre:
mpſſes.And thep to make like proceſſe apeſt onp man ther
of endited afore thepm of onp of the prempſſes.as thep ſhol
de or owbe to doo apenſt onp man that were indpted afore
thepm of onp Ypotte or treſpaſſe.and to determpne it. And
pf onp man be founde gpltp / afore thepm of onp of · the pre:
mpſſes to forfepte the forſapd pepne of a hudred poude. Pe:
ſerupng to the chirche / this punpſſemente notwbpthſton:
dpng the correction of their ſoules acordpng to the lawbes of
the ſame.
　　　　　　⦿ Eſchaunge and rechaũge

⦿ Item for aſmoche as there hath growben/ ꝫ daily grow
eth grete dpſplepſur of god . and grete hurte of the kpnge
our ſouerepn lorde/ and to this his reame.by ꝫ for thpnor:
dpnate chaunges ꝫ rechaũges that haue ben of long tpme
bſed/and pet contpnued in this ſapd reame.wbpthout aucto
rpte gpuen of the kpng to ſuche chaungpng and rechaun:
gpnge ·　　　　　　For remedp wberof many noble ſtatutes
apenſt made .　　　　Wberof one eſpecpall ſtatute made
in the fpftene pere of kpnge Edwarde the thprde

made for the same remedie · in Henry the fourth Henry
the .v. and henry the sixthis dayes wherfore the kyng our sa
yd soueraygn lord wylle. that all suche statutes be put in due
execucyon fromhensforth/ And that noo man make ony ex
chauge without the kyngis licence. ne make ony exchauge
oz rechaunge. of money to be payed wythin this londe/ But
oonly but suche as the kyng shall depute therunto . to kepe
make & aunswere suche exchauges & rechaunges vpon the
peynes in the same statute of kynge Richarde conteyned/
And ouer that it is ordeyned by the kyng our soueraygn lor;
de by thassent of the lordis spirituell & temporell & comens
in his sayd parliament assembled / and by auctoryte of the
same/ that all vnlefull chenysaunces & vsurie be dampned.
and none to be vsed vpon peyn of forfeyture of the value of
the money oz goodes soo cheueschyd or lent the same forfeitu
re to rene vpon the seller oz lener therof ¶ Also for asmo;
che as dyuerse englisshe brokers & estraugers brokers why;
che ben named & assigned to occupye lefull broeage ben In;
ducers & bargayn makers of vnlefull chenysaunce & vsurie
and in some part of vnlefull exchauges to the hurt of our
said soueraygne lord & this his sayd reame. Therfor it is en
acted & stablisshed by p sayd auctorite that all suche brokers
vsing vnlawfully/ of ony of the premysses be put a parte
& neuer to ocupie as brokers within this his reame as thei
maye be aspied & foude in cytees burghs & townes. By may
res baylliffes or ony of theym or of their mynysters where
suche bargen is vsed/ And that euery broker that is foun;
de defectyf. in makynge of vnlawfull brokage / shall for;
fepte/ for euery defaute xx. poude/ And haue enprysone
mente of halfe pere. And ferthermore to be punysshed by
the pilorie/ or otherwyse to their open rebuke and shame. the

kyng to haue thone halfe/of euery of the sayd forfeytures
And the partie that wylle sue thother halfe/of the same by
action of dette/by the comen lawe/And the defendaut in the
same action be not admytted to his lawe ne esson ne protec
cyon be for the same defendaunt alowed/

¶ Concernyng custumers/

¶ Item the kyng our souereyne lord by thadupse & assent
of the lordis spirituell & temporell & the comens assembled
in his sayd parliament/and by auctorite of the same hathe
ordeyned & enacted.that euery marchaunt aswell denyszen
as stranger whiche shall brynge fromhensforth ony maner
of goodes in to ony port wythin this his reame by wey of
marchaudyse.and there do entre the sayd goodes or marcha
undises in the bokes of the custumers of the sayd port whe
re the goodes or marchaudises shall firste come to/And the
kyngis dutie therof to the said custumers contented or ther
fore with hym agreed)And afterward that doon wyll con
ueye or care the same goodes or marchaudises fromthens
in to ony other port wythin the sayd reame.That thene the
owner of the sayd goodes & marchaudises his factour or at
tourney shall bryng from the custumers of the porte where
the sayd goodes or marchaudises be soo entred a certifycat
vnder the same custumers seales direct to the custumers of
the porte wheruto the sayd goodes or marchaudises shall be
coueyed or caried makyng mencyon within the same certifi
cat aswell of the naturell colour length & valure of all ma
ner of marchaudises so entred/vsed to be met wyth elne or
perde as of the naturell weyght content or valure of al ma
ner other marchaudises vsed to be wered or valured And y
the same certificat so made be deliuered to the said custumers
before the sayd goodes be discharged / soo that they maye see

Whether the nature coloure length/Value content or weyght
of the same/doo agree/Wyth the sayd certifycat/soo that the
kynge be not defrauded of his custumes & subsidies therof
due/And yf ony certifycat fromensforth be made by ony cuſ
tumer of ony port Wherwith ony suche marchandiſes. or go
des ſhall be firſt brought vnto/and there in their bokes en=
tred/not makyng mencyon accordyng/as is aforsayd·that
thene the said custumer or customers for their myſbyhaupn=
ge loſe their offyce/and to make fyne With the kyng for the
same at his pleyſur/ And ferthermore if ony suche goodes
or marchaudyſes or ony parcell therof be discharged vnpaki
ked or put to sale Wpthin ony porte than Wpthin the same
Where they ſhall be firſt entred byfore the sayd certifycat be
deliuered / and the same goodes & marchaudiſes seen accor=
dyng as a boue is expreſſed. That thene all the sayd goodes
or marchaudyſes be forfeyted to the kyng our souerayn lord
thone halfe therof to remayne/to his highnes/and thother
half. to him or theym Which ſhall proue ony suche godes or
marchaudiſes soo forfeited. And that the custumer or cuſ=
tumers nor no depute to ony suche comen officer / to Whom
suche certifycat ſhall come/take noo thyng for the sight of
the same godes soo certefied/   Also it is ordeyned & eſtabli
ſhed by auctorite aforsaid/that noo maner of marchaut de=
nyſzen ne ſtrauger do take vpon hym to do entre or cause
to be entred in the bokes of ony custumer of ony port With
in this reame/ony maner marchadises compyng in this his
sayd reame or goyng out of the same. in ony other marcha
utes name/Sauyng oonly the name of the true marchaut
oWner of the same/vpon peyn of forfeiture of al suche godes
& marchaudiſes ſo entred/And eueri of the sayd marchau
tes Whiche ſo ſhal take vpon him to cause suche vntrue etre

to be made to haue prisonement and make fyne therfore/at
the kynges pleasure/And that noo persone take vpon hym
to be custumer coutroller or sercheour in eny porte in ony cy=
te Borugh or towne where he is comen offycer nor noo depu
te to ony suche comen officer vpon peyn of forfeiture for eue
ry halfe yere.that he occuppeth the sayd comen office & offi=
ce of custumership coutroller or sercheour the some of xl.li.
thone halfe therof to the kyng/and thother half to hym that
wylle sue for it by wryttE bylle or informacion ?

Emplopement

¶ Item that where in the parliament of kyng Edwarde
the iiij.holden at Westmynster the vij.yere of his wygne /It
was ordeyned among other that euery marchaut alien and
euery other Viteler & other estraunger not beynge denszein
that resorte to ony place or porte wythin this reame or Wa
les after the fest of Ester thene next folowyng sholde duely
enploye/all the monep by hym to be reserued wythin ony
porte wythin this reame or Wales vpon the marchandyses
or other comodytees of this reame/or elles wythout frau=
de put the same money in due payment wythin this reame
the same enplopemet or payment duely to be proued by the
marchat Viteler or other estranger before his departyng ou
te of the same porte by wrytyng fro that marchaut or mar=
chautes to whom the sayd marchaut alien Viteler or other es
trauger haue enploped or payed his monep by hym recep=
ued for his marchaudyses brought in to this londe . Wyt=
nessynge that he hathe soo doon.or elles by suche proues as
shall be thought resonable/to the custumer or coutroller of the
same portes or to the mayre baylluf or other chief gouerners
of ony cyte Borugh or towne where suche port shall be.Vp
on peyne of forfeiture of all his goodes beyng wythin this

rrame. and to haue enprpſonement of a peïe ſaupng to eue
ry ſucïe marchannt Bptelïer ꝗ otïher eſtrauͤger his reſonaẞe
coſtes. Ꝟopth certepn prouipions iṇ the ſame. as Bp the ſame
actïe more at large ꝟooth appere. Ꝟhicïe actïe ꝟas maꝺe to
enꝺure / But oonlp from the ſapꝺ feſt of Eſter to the enꝺe of
Ꞡꝟ. peres tïhene next ſuping / Soo that noo golꝺe ꝗ ſiluer re
cepued Bp marchauͤtes aliens ꝗ otïher Bptelꝺers ꝗ eſtrangeres
not ꝭepng ꝺpnſzens for marchauͤdiſe Brought iṇ to this lõ
ꝺe is not emploped Bpon the comodïtees of this lonꝺe. But
conuepeꝺ ꝗ caried out of this rrame to the grete loſſe to the
ꝭpng. of his cuſtume ꝗ ſuẞſidie / and enpouerſïhpng of this
rrame   It is enacïteꝺ orꝺepneꝺ ꝗ eſtaẞliſïheꝺ Bp the ꝭpnge
our ſouerepn lorꝺ that noꝟ is / Bp thaꝺupres of the lorꝺis ſpi
rituell ꝗ temporell / and at the praper of the comens iṇ this
ſaiꝺ parliament aſſẽẞleꝺ / ano Bp auctoritïe of the ſame / that
the ſapꝺ actïe maꝺe the ſapꝺ ꝟꝟꝵ. pere of the reigne of ꝭpn
ge Eꝺꝟard the iiꝵ. Ꝟopth all thpnges compriſeꝺ iṇ tïhe ſa=
me / touchpnge the prempſſees. ano euerp prouipion maꝺe iṇ
the ſame ꝭe good effectuell ꝗ to enꝺure for euer / ℂ Alſo
it is enacïteꝺ Bp the ſaid auctoritïe / that eueri marchauͤt of Jr
relonꝺe / Jerneſep or Garneſſep that Brpngeth onp marchauͤ
diſe iṇ to this rrame ſïhall enplop tïhe monep recepueꝺ for tïhe
ſame marchauͤdiſe. his reſonaẞe expſpences ꝺeꝺuct) Bpon the
comodïtees of this lonꝺe / or elles ꝟopthout frauꝺe put tïhe ſa
me monep iṇ due papment ꝟopthin this rrame / Tïhe ſaid en
ploplment or papment to ꝭe proueꝺ as is aforſapꝺ / Bpoṇ pp
ne of forïepture of the Ꞡalue of the marchauͤdiſe ſo Brough
tïe iṇ this lonꝺe. ℂ Ano it is orꝺepneꝺ Bp the ſapꝺ aucto=
ritïe that euerp cuſtumer or coutroller ſïhall take ſufficpentïe
ſuertie / for euerp of the ſapꝺ marchauͤt Bitelïer or otïher eſtra
unger to enplope. tïhe Ꞡalue of tïhe ſapꝺ marchauͤdiſes. or to

ℂ   ꝵ.

put the same monei for ye marchaūdise receiued in due paimēt
his resonable expences allwaye deducte. Vpon peyn of forfei
ture of the value/of the sayd marchaūdyses. thone halfe of
the sayd forfeiture/to the kyng/ thother halfe to the partye
that wylle sue/ This to begynne & take effecte at the fest of
Cristemasse nexte comyng/

¶ Ayenst the ordynaūce of london of goyng to feyres/
¶ Item it was shewed vnto the kyng our sayd souereyn
lorde by a petityon put vnto hym/in his sayd parliamente.
that how of late tyme/ the Mayre aldermen & citezeins of ye
citee of london/ haue made an ordenaūce wythin the same ci
tee vpon a grete payn/ that noo man that is a free man or
citezein of the sayd citee/ shal go or come at ony feyre or mar
ket oute of the sayd citee of london with ony maner of wa
re or marchaūdyse. to selle or to bartre/ to this entente/ that
all byers & marchaūtes shold resorte to the sayd cytee. to bie
their ware & marchaūdyses of the sayd citezeins & free men
at london aforsayd/ by cause of theyr synguler lucre & avay
le. The kynge our souereyn lorde in consideracyon of the
hurt likly to growe. of & by the premysses: hath by the aduy
se & assent of the lordis spirytuell & temporell . and the com
mens in his sayd parliament assembled/ and by auctoryte
of the same. ordeyned stablisshed & enacted/ that euery free-
man & citezen of the sayd citee of london that now is or here
after shall be/ may fre carye & goo wyth his or their by vay-
le ware or marchaūdyse/ whatsoeuer it be/ at his or their li
bertee/ to ony fayre & market that shall please hym or theim
wythin this reame of Englonde. ony statute act or ordena
ūce made or to be made within the sayd citee of london to the
contrarie of the premysses not wythstondyng.   And the
sayd ordenaūce & acte made in the said citee/ be voyde and of
none effecte/ And that noo persone of the sayd cite/ be hurte

nor preiudised in losyng of his libertie a frauchise wythin þ
sayd cite or otherwyse by reason or occasion of anullynge
of the said ordenaunce and acte or for none obeyng to thef
fecte of the same/ And yf ony persone be preiudyced in ony
wyse. by occasion of the same/ that he that putteth or causeth
ony persone to suche preiudyce/ loose a forfeyte to the kynge
v.li. as ofte as he soo doth/ And he that wylle sue for suche
forfeyture/ haue therfore an action of dette apenst suche of
fender/ the kyng to haue execucyon of thone halfe/ and he þ
sueth thother halfe/ And in suche action the defendaunte be
not amytted to wage his lawe .

⸿ Domage geuen in a writ of errour

⸿ Item that where of ten times pleyntyf or demaudaunte
pleyntfs demaundautes that haue iugement to recouere/ be
delaied of execucyon for that the defendaunt or tenaut defen
dautes or tenautes apenst whom iugement is gyuen. or o
ther that ben bounde by the sayd iugement/ sueth a wryt or
writtes of errour to adnulle a reuerse/ the sayd iugement to
thentent oonly to delay execucyon of the sayd iugement.
It is enacted ordeyned a stablished by thadupse of the lor
dis spirituell a temporell. and at the prayer of the comens
in the sayd parliament assembled. and by auctorytie of the sa
me/ that yf ony suche defendaunt or tenaute defendautes or
tenautes/ or yf ony other that shall be bounde/ by the sayd iu
gement sue afore execucyon hade ony wryt of errour to re
uerse ony suche iugement in delaying of execucyon. that the
ne yf the same iugement be affermed good. in the sayd writ
of errour a not erroneus or that the sayd writ of errour be
dyscontynued in the defaute of the partie/ or that persone
or persones that sueth wrytte or wryttes of errour be
nounsued in the same that thenne the sayd persone or perso

c   ij

nes ayenſt Whom/the ſayd Writ of errour is ſued ſhall reco
uere his coſtes & domage/for his delay and wrongfull Rep:
acyon in the ſame by diſcrecion of the iuſtyces afore whom
the ſayd Writ of errour is ſued.

❡ Clothes to be caried ouer the ſee. be barbed rowed and
ſhorne except. &c.

❡ Item where in the ſayd parliament it was ſhewed by the
comen fullers & other artifycers that ſholde liue and opteyn
their nedy ſuſtentacyon by meane of draperie/ made & dra:
ped wythin this reame. aſwell thorugh out the ſame rea:
me. as wythin the cyte of london. that where as in a ſtatu:
te made the ij. yere of the reygne of kyng edwarde the iiij.
amonges other: it is conteyned / that noo perſone denſ3en
ne ſtraůger ſhold carie or doo to be caried to ony parties be:
yonde the ſee/ ony woollen yerne/ nor cloth Vnfulled. But the
Woollen yerne to be made in this reame. ſholde be wouen in the
ſame/ And alſo all cloth in the ſame made. ſholde be fulled &
fully wrought wythin this reame before that ony of the
ſame ſholde be had or caried oute of this reame Vpon peyne
of forfeyture of the euery Value of ſuche yerne/ not wouen
and clothe not fulled/had or caried oute of this reame/the
one halfe of the ſame forfeyture to be keuped to thuſe of the
kyng.and that other halfe of it/ to hym or theym that ſhold
eſpye or malie proue of ony ſuche yerne not wouen or clo:
the not fulled/caried to ony place beyonde the ſee/   And
for aſmoche as in the ſayd ſtatute of kyng Edwarde/there
is none expreſſe mencyon made that the ſayd clothes ſhold
be rowed and ſhorne. afore that they be caried and conueid
oute of this reame/Wherby the ſayd poure comens of the
craftes aforeſayd myght be ſette in labour and occupacyon
therfore the ſayd clothes euer ſithen in to this daye/haue be

and yet daily arne·in grete nombre and plente caryed & con
ueyed out of this reame Vnwroied and shorne/ in to the par
tie of beyonde the see/as well by denyzens as straungers
Wherby oure londysshe nacions Wyth the same drapery·arne
set in labour and ocupacion to their grete enriching/and the
pour comens of the craftes abouesaid/thrugh al this reame
that of naturell reason/ as the kyngis true liege men sholde
haue·& opteyn their nedy sustentacon & leuing bi meanes of
the same draperi·for lacke of suche ocupacyon dayly fall·in
grete nombre·in to idelnes & pouerte/ to their Vttermost dest
ruction·if it shold only lenger contynue   The kyng our sayd
souerein lord the premysses consideren·By thaduyse of the lor
des spirituell & temporell·and at the prayer of the comens in
his sayd parliament assembled & By auctorite of the same/
hath ordeined establisshed & enacted that noo strauger nor de
niszen carie or make to be caried out of this reame/ only Wol
len clothes But that they before be barbed rowed & shorn Wyth
in this same reame/ for the releef & settyng on Werke of the
sayd pour comens/Vpon the peyn & forfepture limpted in the
said statute·of king edward/ made Vpon clothes caried out
of this reame not fulled tobe deuided in maner & fourme as
in the same statute it is contepned/Prouyded allway that clo
thes called Vesses rapes sapling clothes & all other clothes co
menly solde at xl·shelinges & Vnder be not coprised in thys
present acte/   ¶ Retepnoour
¶ Item the kyng remeembryng how by the necligence & Vn
laWful demenynges of stuardes auditours receyuours sur
ueiours & Baylifs of his honours lordshpps maners londis
& tenementis constables & keprs of castelles Wardeins ma
isters of game & kepers of his forestis chaces parkes & Wa
rens Wythin this his reame ·grete Vnsuertie hath groWen

afore this tyme/aswell to his highnes/as to his progenytours.and how his tenautes & inhabytantes of his sayd honours lordshyppe manoyrs londes & tenementes dayly ben gretly troubled/aswell by thunlawfull retepners & retyrewowes made aswell by the sayd officers. and suffryng the same tenautes & inhabitauntes to be vnlawfully retepned wyth other persones/And how by this vnlawfull retepnyng thei ben called to vnlawfull assembles & riottes to their oft gre te ieopdies & charges. Wherby they ben soo enpouersshd that they ben not of power to pay to hym their duties. and his subgettes nere their dwellyng ben vexed & troubled & gretly hurt bi dyuers charges & vnlawfull imposicions/And o= uer this his highnes remembreth how his wooders his vert & venyson by the wardeyns maysters of the game.parkes kepers & other officers of his sayd forestes chaces parkes & warrens thrugh out this his reame.is almost destroyed And that dyuers & many persones to whom he hath grauted suche offices in his grete troubles had apenst his traito urs & rebelles haue absented them from his grace contrari to the dutie of their alegeaunce & apenst all trouth & kynones Wherfore the kyng our souerayn lord wyll that.by thadup= ce & assent of the lordis spirituell & teporell/and the comes in this his sayd parliament assembled/ and by auctorite of the same/it be ordeyned & enacted that if ony stuarde audito ur recepuour suruepour or Baylsif. that now is or herafter shall be/of ony of the said honours lordshipe manoyrs lon= des & tenementes constable or keper of ony of his sayd cas= telles/wardepn mayster of game/parkes keper or ony other officer of ony of his sayd forestes chaces parkes or war= rens that now is or herafter shall be/be vnlawfully retep= ned with ony persone/froshensforth. or retein ony man dwel

ling Wpthin ony of the sapd honours lordships maners lo
des & tenementes. contrari to ony ordenauce or act afore this
tyme made/ or suffre ony man dwelling Wpthin the sapd ho
noures lordships maners londes & tenementis to be Bnlaw
fully retepned Wpth ony other man or persone What degre
or condpcion soeuer he be of · And shewe it not to the kynge
Wpthin yl. dapes next after he hath knowlecke therof. And
how & With whom he is soo retepned/ Or ony of the sapd of
ficers conuey ony of the sapd tenautes inhabitautes fermo
urs to the kyng/to ony felde or assemble or route· other Wpse
than by the kyngis comaudement to doo hym suche serupse
as he shall be comauded/ And that allwap in the kyngis li=
uere or signe/Wpth a conpsauce of hym/that soo conuey the=
pm by the kyngps comaudement/ Or pf suche offpcer come
not to y kyngis highnes in tyme of trouble· or werre/ Wha
he therto shall be comauded hauyng noo resonable excuse/to
the contrarie/that all grautes than made. or had to hym/of
ony of the sapd offices by the kyng/ or by ony of the kyn=
gis progenytours or predecessours. be thene Btterly Boyde &
of none effect/ And it is ordepned by the same auctorite
that if ony fermour or tenaut Wpthin ony of the sapd hono
urs lordships maners londes & tenementes be retepned With
ony persone or persones. contrarie to the statutes by liueree.
signe token or oth indenture or prompse/ Or to goo to ony
felde gadrpng or assemble . in ony mannps liueree. signe or
token/But oonlp in the kyngis liuere & signe . and to serue
hpm oonlp. or Where he shall be comauded by the kyng/ that
all grautes & leses to hpm made for terme of yeres or at the
Wpsse/of londes tenementes rentes or other possessions be=
png parcell of ony of the sapd honours lordships maners
londes & tenemetes/be thene Btterly Boyde & of none effect/

⸿ Item for asmoche as the grete and auncient defence of this reame hath stonde by tharchers & shooters in longbowes/whiche is now left & fallen in decay for the derth & excessiff price of longbowes / It is therfore ordeyned & establisshed by the kynge our souereyn lord/ by thaduys of the lordis spirituell & temporell & assent of the comens in the sayd parliament assembled/and by auctorite of the same.that yf ony persone or persones after the fest of the Purifycacyon of our lady nexte comyng selle ony longe bowe/ouer the price iij. shelinges iiij. that thene the seller or sellers of suche bowe forfeyt for euery bowe so solde ouer the sayd price vl. shelynges.to the kyng. And he that wylle sue for the same haue an action of dette therfore.ayenst suche seller.or make informacion in the kyngis eschequer therof/ the kyng to haue execucion of the moyte therof/ and he that sueth thother moyte) And that in suche action of dette. the deffendaut haue noo assoigne ne protection for hym alowed./ and be not admytted to wage his lawe/

⸿ Felonye

⸿ Item for asmoche as by quarelles made to suche as have the ken in grete auctorite office & of counceyll wyth kyngis of this reame/hath ensued the destruction of the kyngis & the neer vndoyng of this reame soo as it hath apperid euydently. when compassyng of the deth of suche as were of the kyngis true subgettes was had/the destruccyon of the prynce was ymagened therby. And for the most partie it hath growen & ben occasioned by enuye & malice of the kyngis owne howshol de seruautes/as now late lyke thyng was lykly to haue ensued/ And for somoche as by the law of this londe yf actuell dede be not had / there is noo remedye for suche false compassynges ymagynacions & confederacyes

had agayn ony lord or ony of the kynges coũseill or ony of
the kynges grete officers in his houshold. as stewarde treso
rer coũptroller.and so grete incõuenyences myght ensue of
suche Vngoodly demeanyng sholo not be straitly punysshed/
or thactuel dede there won/Therfore it is ordeyned By ỹ kin
ge the lordes spirituell & tẽporel & the comens in the sayd par
liament assembled & By auctorite of the same/that frõhensfo
urthwarde/the stewarde tresourer & cõptroller of the kyngys
hous for the tyme being/or one of theim haue full auctorite
& power to enquere.By xij.sad & discrete psones of the cheki
ker roll of the kynges honourable houshold/if ony seruaũte
admytted to be his seruaũt sworn & his name put in to the
chekiker roll of his housholde whatsoeuer he be seruing in o
ny maner office or wome.reputed had & take vnder the sta
te of a lord.make ony confederacies compassynges conspy-
racies ymagynacions wyth ony psone or persones to destro
ye or murdre the kynge or ony lord of this reame or ony o
ther persone sworn to the kynges coũseill/stuwarde tresorer
cõptroller of the kynges hous/that if it be foũde/afore the sa
yd stuarde.for the tyme beyng By the sayd xij.sad men.that o
ny suche of the kynges seruaũtes as is aboue said/hath cõ
federed compassed comprised or ymagened/as is aboue sayd
that he so foũde/Bi that enquerry/be put therupon to answer
And the stuarde tresourer & comptroller or ij.of theim haue
power to determyne the same mater,accordyng to the lawe
And if he put hym in triell/that thẽne it be tried Bi other xij
sad men of the same housholde. And that suche mysdoers ha
ue noo chalenge/But for malice/& if suche mysdoers be fo-
ũde gilty/By confession or otherwyse.that the sayd offence be
iudged felony.And they to haue Iugement & execucion as
felons attepnted owe to haue By the comen lawe/

¶ Expiratur

¶ Item for asmoche as afore tyme dyuerse persones feof/
fees of trust. and other whiche haue sued actions or sutes
to thuse of other persone or persones/and not to their vse ne
behoue haue be disabled to sue suche action or sute. And som
tyme barred in the same. By the reason that tho persones soo
suyng ben outlawed of treson felony or otherwyse/Attayn
ted coupeted or otherwyse dysabled to their grete delay & hur
te of thos persones to whos vse behoue & profyt the same ac
cion or actions soo were sued or had. It is ordeyned esta=
blisshed & enacted by the kyng our souereyn lord/by thassent
of the lordis spirituell & temporell/and the comens in this
present parliament assembled/ no by auctorite of the same
that noo persone or persones whiche now hathe or herafter
shall haue ony action or sute hangyng. to thuse & behoue of
other persones than of theymself. be not fromhensfforth dys=
abled ne excluded to pursue the same actions or sutes/and
execucion of the same to effecte by ony outlawry attaynder
or conuyction/But that thoo persones soo suing may mayn
tene & pursue the same actions or sutes wyth lawfull exe=
cucions of the same. And thos persones to whos vse ony
suche thyng shall be recouered or had/ shal mowe haue and
enioye the same. the sayd outlawryes attaynders or conuyc
cyons notwythstondyng / This acte to endure vnto the
nexte parliament.

TO the worſhip of god and of all holy chirche/And for the comen welt e proffyt of this reame of Eng: lond/ Our ſouereyn lord Henry By the grace of god kyng of Englonde e of fraūce and lord of Irlonde the Bij. after the conqueſte at his parliament holden at Weſtmynſter the viij. daye of Januarye/in the fourth yere of his regne/ By thaduys e aſſent of the lordis ſpirituell e temporell/and the comens in the ſayd parliament aſſembled/and by aucto rite of the ſame/hath won to be made ordeyned e ſtablyſhed dyuerſe ſtatutes e ordenaūces in fourme that foloweth.

¶ For commyſſyons of Sewers

¶ Firſt it was ſhewed by the comens in the ſayd parli ament aſſembled that Where in the parliament of the right no ble prynce Henry the Bj.late kyng of englond holden at Weſt mynſter.the Bj. yere of his regne.the conſidered grete hurr tes e loſſes Whiche then were by thencreace of water in di uers parties of this reame / and many gretter hurtes likly ſhold haue come yf remedye in that behalfe. ſhold not haſtly haue be puruayd/ It was enacted ordeyned e ſtablyſhed/By auctorite of the ſame parliament.that for p.yeres than nex te folowyng.ſeuerall commyſſions of ſewers ſholde be made to dyuers perſones by the chaūceler of englond for the tyme beyng. to be named in dyuerſe parties of this reame.Where newe were.after the fourme e tenour of a commyſſion in the ſa id acte ſpecifyed/And afterwarde in the parliamet of the ſa id late kyng holden at Weſtmynſter the Biij. yere of his regne/ By cauſe the commyſſioners named in the ſayd commyſſion had not playn power ne auctorite to doo perfourme e exe cute thinges compriſed in the ſaid commyſſion / It was ordey ned e ſtablyſhed br thauctorite of the ſame parliamet that al ſuche commyſſioners ſhold haue power to make e execute ſta tutes 7 ordenaūces after efect e purport of p ſaid commyſſion

And after the said y. yeres past in the parlyament of the sa
id late kyng/holden at Westmynster the xviij. yere of his re;
igne. It was also ordeyned enacted & stablisshed By auctorite
of the same parliament/that for x. yeres than next folowyn
ge severall commyssions of sewers sholde be made to dyverse
persones by the chaunceler of england for the tyme being/to be
named in all parties of this reame/Where nede sholde be/af;
ter the sayd fourme & effect of the sayd commission conteyned
in the sayd act/made the said vj. yere/And that suche commis
sioners shold have power to ordeyne & execute statutes & or
denaunces & other thynges doo after theffect & purport of the
said commyssions/ And afterwarde in the parliament of the
said late kyng holden at Westmynster the xviij. yere of his
reygne/It was also ordeyned enacted & stablisshed/by auctori
te of the same parliament/that for yv. yeres than next folow
yng/the chaunceler of england for the tyme beyng shold have
power to make out of the chauncerie commyssions of sewers
vnder the grete seale /in suche fourme as it was graunted to
be made/by the said act made/the sayd vj. yere/as in the said act
is more playnly conteyned / And after the sayd xv. yeres
passed in the parliament of the noble prynce edwarde the fo
urth/late kyng of england holden at Westmynster the rij. ye
re of his reygne/It was also ordeyned enacted & stablisshed/
By auctorite of the same parliament/that for yv. yeres than
next folowyng/severall commyssions of sewers shold be made
to dyvers psones by the chaunceler of england for the tyme be
ynge to be named in all parties of this reame & also of the
marches of calais guynes & hames/Where nede shold be after
the fourme & effect of the said commyssion conteyned in the said
acte/made in the said vj yere. And that all suche commps;
sioners shold have full power to make ordeyne and execute

ſtatutes ꝛ oꝛdenaunces and otheꝛ thynges to do afteꝛ thef
fecte ꝛ puꝛporte of the ſame cōmpſſions/as in the ſame act
moꝛe pleynly is contepned/Bi Whiche cōmpſſions ꝛ auctori
te peuen to the ſaid cōmpſſioners in the ſayd fourme many
gꝛete huꝛtes ꝛ incōuenyētes in dpuerſe paꝛties of this ꝛra
me wyn ꝛ had bi ēcreſe of Water Weꝛe neceſſacely ꝛewꝛſſed ꝛe
fourmed ꝛ amended/Jt is ſo noW that late aſWell in the co
ūties of gloceſtꝛe ꝛ ſomerſet as elles Wheꝛe in dpuerſe paꝛtp
es of this ꝛeame.ꝛ alſo Wythin the boūdes of the ſayd mar;
ches of calays guyſnes ꝛ hāmes/By thencreaſe of Wateꝛs
dpuers londes ꝛ tenementes in gꝛete quantite ben ſuꝛouūded
ꝛ deſtwoyed/and many moo gꝛete like huꝛtes ꝛ dōmages be
like Wythin ſhort tyme to fal/aſWell to the decreace ꝛ deſtruc
cyon of the liuelood of the kyng ouꝛ ſoueꝛeyn loꝛd as of the
liuelood of the chiꝛche ꝛ of otheꝛ true lige pꝛple of this ꝛeame
and of the ſayd marches ꝛ anpentiſment of the ſame.Wyth;
out that ꝛemedye in that behalf/be puꝛueyed ꝛ had/The kin
ge ouꝛ ſayd ſoueꝛeyn loꝛd theꝛfoꝛe of his mooſt habūdanut
grace.the pꝛempſſes tendꝛly conſideꝛd bi thaduyſe ꝛ aſſent
of the loꝛdes ſpirituell ꝛ tempoꝛell/and at the ꝛequeſt of the
comens in the ſayd parliament aſſembled.and by auctoꝛpte
of the ſame parliament/hath oꝛdepned enacted ꝛ ſtabliſſhed
that foꝛ yꝛb.peꝛes next compng ſeuerall comiſſions of ſelw
eꝛs be made to dpuerſe perſones.Bi the chaūceler of Englon
de foꝛ the tyme being to be named in all paꝛties of this his
ꝛeame ꝛ of the ſayd marches Wheꝛe nede is or ſhall be. afteꝛ
the fourme ꝛ effecte of the ſayd cōmpſſion/contepned in the
ſayd acte made in the ſayd Bij.peꝛe/   ❡ And oueꝛ
that hath oꝛdepned and ſtabliſſhed by the ſayd auctoꝛpte
that all ſuche Commpſſyoners haue full poWer to make
oꝛdepne and execute ſtatutes and oꝛdenaunces and

other thynges do after theffecte & purport of the same compl
spon/

¶ Item where as it was of olde tyme vsed & contynued
tyll now of late yeres/that there was for the auayle of the
kyng & the reame fynours & parters of golde & siluer by fi
re & water vnder a rule & order/belonging vnto the myntes
of london/ calays/caunterbery.porke. & durham.and in other
places where myntes were holden / and at the goldsmythis
hall in london to fyne & part all golde & siluer belongyng or
nedefull for the sayd myntes & felishyp of goldsmythis for
thadmendements of moneys & plate in the reame/that eue
ry thyng/myght be reformed to the right standarde aswel
in moneys as plate.to the leest cost/for the wele of the kyn
gis noble men of the londe & comen people. But soo it is
now/that suche fynours & parters of golde & siluer by fyre
& water/dwellen abrode in euery place of the reame.oute of
the rules aforsayd/and bie gylte siluer from the myntes cha
unges & goldsmythys.and parte & fyne it as is aforsayd
And for the moost parte/the siluer soo fyned.they do alay
it in dyuerse maners. and selle it at their plesure to euery
man that wylle bye it of theym / to make suche werkes as
pleyseth the byers.Therfore men canne gete noo fyne siluer
whan they nede it/for their money/for thadmendements of
money & plate as hath ben in tymes passed.wherfore it cau
seth money & plate / in dyuerse places of the reame. to be
made werse in fynesse/than it sholde be.as it appereth euyden
tly in diuers places to the grete hurt of y kingis noble men
of the londe & comen peple/wherfore the kyng our said soue
rein lord/bi thassent of the lordis spirituel & temporell and
comens in this sayd parliament assembled/& by auctorite of
the same. hath ordeyned establisshed and enacted / that noo

fynour of golde and ſiluer nor parter of the ſame/ By fyre
or water from henſforth alaye ne fyne ſiluer nor golde nor
none ſelle in ony other wyſe/Ne to ony perſone or perſones
But oonly to thofficers of myntes chaūges τ goldſmythis
wythin this reame. for augmentacion τ amendyng of coig
ne τ plate as aforſayd/ And that the mayſters of myntes
chaūges τ goldſmythes for all ſuche fyne golde or ſiluer co
myng to theym. to anſwere the Balour as it is worth acor
dyng as it is now τ hath ben of aūcient tyme accuſtomed
after the rate of fynes/ Ne that noo fynour nor fynours/
parter nor parters ſelle to no perſone neyther to one ne to o?
ther ony maner of ſiluer in maſſe molton τ alayed Bpon pe
yn of forfeyture of the ſame. the kyng therof to haue thone
halfe/and the fynder that can proue. and wyll ſue it in the
kyngis eſchequer thother half/And if ony fynour or fyno
urs parter or parters of golde τ ſiluer either bi fire or water
alaye or ſelle ony fyne ſiluer or golde otherwyſe than it is
ordeyned in this laſte acte / he or they to leaſe the Balour of
the ſame golde or ſiluer ſoo alayed or ſolde/ the kynge ther?
of to haue the one halfe. and the fynder that can proue it τ
wylle ſue it in the kynges eſchequer the other halfe . Alſo
all ſuche fyne ſiluer as ſhall be parted τ fyned/as is afore?
ſayd/that it be made ſoo fyne. that it maye bere pij. peny wer
pght of alaye in a pounde wight/ and yet it be as good as
ſterling and rather better than worſe/And that euery fyno
ur put his ſeuerall marke/Bppon ſuche fyne ſylu er/ to bere
wytneſſe to the ſame/ to be true as is aforeſayd/ Bpon the
peyne of the Balure founde contrarye to be forfeyte. the kyng
therof to haue thone half.and the fynder that can proue it τ
will ſue it in the eſchequer thother halfe/   Alſo that noo
                                            goldſmith

goldsmythis wythin this reame/ melt oz alay ony fyne sil
uer to ne for ony werkers or other entent/But onely for ma
kyng of amelles for dyuerse werkes of goldsmythrie /and
foz amendyng of plate to make it as good as sterlinge/or
better/for the comen wele of this reame (Nor that they selle
noo fyne siluer nor other siluer alayed molten in to masse/
to ony persone or persones whatsoeuer they be/nor one gold
smyth to a nother. This ordenauce to be kept by the gold
smythis in euery poynt vpon peyn of forfeyture of the sa:
me siluer oz valure therof/The kyng therof to haue the one
halfe / and the fynder that can proue it & wyll sue it in the
kyngis eschequer thother half. ⸿ Also it is ozdeyned by
the same auctorite that all lettres patentes & grauntes of of
fyces belongyng oz perteynynge to the mynte of our souere
yn lord the kyng exercised in the same wyth fees & wages
therto belongyng. be fromhensforth voide/& of none effect /

⸿ Ayenst Bochers .

⸿ Item it was shewed by a pticyon put to the kyng our
sayd souereyn lorde in the sayd parliameut by his subgettes
& paryshens of the parisshe of saynt Feythes & saynt Gre:
gories in londoñ nygh adioynaut vnto the cathedrall chir
che of Powles /that it was soo that grete concourse of pe:
ple as well of hys ryall persone/as of other grete lordes and
astates wyth other his true subgettes often tymes was
had vnto the sayd chathedrall chirche/and for the most par
te thorugh oute the parisshe aforesayd/ the whiche often ty:
mes ben gretly ennoyed & inuenimed by corrupt eires enge
dred in the sayd parisshes by occasion of bloode & other foul
ler thynges.by occasion of the slaughter of bestes & scaldin
ge of swyne/had & done in the bocherie/of seynt Nycholas
fleshshamels /whos corrupcyon by violence/ of vnclene and

putrifyed waters is borne downe thrugh the sayd parisshes
and compasseth two partes of the palays Where the kynges
moost ropall persone is woñt to abyde. Whan he cometh to p
cathedrall chirche for ony acte there to be don to the Jubar:
wuse abydyng of his moost noble persone/and to ouer gre:
te ennoisaunce of the parisshens there, and of other the kyn
gis subgettis ε straũgers that passe by the same/ Comple
ynte Wherof at dyuerse ε many seasons almoost by the space
of xvj. peres contynuelly aswell by the chanons ε pety cha
none of the sayd cathedrall chirche/londlordes there/as al
so by many other dyuerse of the kyngis subgettes of right
honest hauiour vnto dyuerse maires ε aldermen of the cite of
london hath be made/and noo remedie had ne foũden/that it
please our said souerepn lorde of his habũdant grace to pro
uyde for the conseruacyon aswell of his moost ropall perso:
ne/ as to socour his pour subgettes ε suppliauntes in this
behalfe/ Consideryge that in few noble citees and tow:
nes or none Wythin cristendome. Where as trauepling men
haue labored/that the comen slaughter hous of bestis sholde
be kept in ony speciall parte Wythin the Walles of the same
leest it myght engender sikenesse. to the destruction of the pe:
ple/ The kyng our said souerepn lord in consideracyon of
the prempsses/hath by thadupse ε assent of the lordis spiri
tuell ε temporell/and the comens in the said parliament af
sembled. and by auctorite of the same. ordepned and stablished
that noo bocher nor his seruaũt slee noo maner best Wythin
the sayd house/called the caldynge house.or Wythin the Wal
les of london. Vpo n peyne to forfepte for euery oxe vij. pens
and euery kowe ε for euery other best viij. pens thone half
therof to the kyng our sayd souerepn lorde. and thother half
to euery of the kyngis lieges that Wylle sue for the same/by

action of dette / And noo protection or essoyne be alowed
to ony of the defendauntes agenst whom ony suche action
shall be conceyued / And that in the same action of dette su
che processe be made as in other actions of dette sued at the
comen lawe/And ouer this it is ordeyned & enacted by the
sayd auctorite that the same ordenauce acte & lawe extende
& be obserued & kepte in euery citie burgh & towne walled
wythin this reame of englonde/and in the towne of cam;
brigge.the townes of berwyke & carlile oonly excepte & for
prised.Prouyded allway that this present acte begyn & take
effecte at the fest of anunciacyon of our lady nexte comynge
and not afore /

　　¶ Protections for passers in to Bretayn

¶ Item the kynge our sayd souereyn lorde for dyuerse cau
ses & resonable consideracyons hym mouyng/by thassent of
the lordes spirituell & temporell & the comes in this present
parliament assembled/and by auctorite of the same hath en
acted ordeyned & stablisshed that euery persone of what condi
cyon or degree he be of/beyng or herafter be/in our sayd soue
reyn lorde the kynges wages beyonde the see in Bretayn at
his pleisure haue the protection of profecturo or moratur cu
clausula Bolum9/And in thexcepcyon of the sayd protecty;
on there be made empssion of assises.And that the sayd pro
tection be alowable in all the kynges courtes/and other co;
urtes where the sayd protections shall be pleded/ or layd for
ony of the sayd persones.in all pleys & assises.aswell of no
uell dissesin as of fresshe force/without ony dyfficultee. Al
so it is enacted that the iudgementes to be geuen from hens
forth in suche assise.arraines or to be arrayned shall not be
preiudicyal to ony of the sayd persones soo beyng in the ser;
uyse of our souereyn lord the. kyng.in Bretayn as is afore,

sapd Whiche haue ony thyng in reuersion or remayndre in
londes ꝭ tenemētes/Wherof suche assise be arrapned/if the na
me of thos persones Whiche ben in the reuersion oꝛ the rema
pndre of suche londes ꝭ tenementes be not in the sapd assise
But that the sapd iugement be apenst all thepm. Bopde. The
sapd ordenaūce to endure ꝭ be auaplable/ to euery of the sa:
pd psones as long as be abpdeth soo in the kynges Wages
And if this ordenaūce touchyng the sapd persones so noW
abidynge/oꝛ that after this shall abpde/in the serupce of the
kpngis highnes in bretein be not sufficient foꝛ thease ꝭ su
ertie of thepm/It is agreed ꝭ accorded By the same auctorite
That our sapd souerepn loꝛde the kyng ꝭ all the loꝛdis of
his coūsepl for the tyme bepng/haue ful poWer in all maner
of actions sutes ꝭ pꝛocesses to gꝛaūt to euerp of suche perso
nes protection/as shall be in their cause auaplable after the
iꝛ descrecyon durpng the tyme that they or ony of thepm con
typnue in the sapd arme or Warre/Pꝛoupded that this act be
not auaplable to ony persone for ony entre sithen the firste
dape of this pꝛesent parliament. Also it is enacted that pf
ony dpscent of ony londes oꝛ tenementes or ony other ri3t
or heredptamētes be to ony persone oꝛ persones bepng Wpth
in this reame or elles Where/that. that discent be of nod gre
ter effect to the dōmages or hurt of the sapd persones bepn
ge in the kpngis serupce/as is aforsapd. Thène pf the said
persones in the kpngis serupce soo bepng Were Wpthin the a
ge of xvj. peres/ Also it is ordepned By the sapd auctorite/
that all suche persones as shall passe ouer the see in the said
Biage/and euery of thepm Whiche haue londes ꝭ tenemētes
holden of the kpng oꝛ of ony other shall moW laWfully ma
ke therof feoffementes ꝭ transmutacion of possessyon By de
de or dedes fyne or fynes recouere oꝛ recoueres for the perso

        d   ij

urmaunce of theyr wylles wythout ony fyne for the sayd feoffement or transmutacion of possession therfore to be made in. And that they & euery of theym/ their heires & assygnes of euery of theym, be dischardged of all suche fynes by the sayd acte wythoute lettres patentes of licence/ or pardon or other dyscharge to be had in that behalue. And ferdermore it is also ordeyned & enacted by the sayd auctorite/that if ony of the sayd persones soo passynge in the sayd Byage whiche holde londes or tenementes of the kyng. or of ony other by knyghtes seruyce or otherwyse. wherfore his heyre oweth to be in warde / and fortune in the sayd Byage to decesse/beyonde the see/or that ony feoffement of the same londes & tenementes be supposed to be made by collusion. theyre of the owner of the same londes and tenementes beyng wythin age. that thenne the feoffes or executoures of suche persone soo deceased haue the warde & mariage of the heyre soo beynge wythin age/and of the londes & tenementes soo holden duryng the nonage of euery suche heyre to the performaunce of the wylle of the sayd persone soo deceased wythout ony accompt or other thyng therfore to be yolden) Prouyded alway/that if ony persone or persones reteyned in the sayd arme or Biage. resorte & come ayen in to this reame discharged of the said retenue armee & Byage or after the said Byage determyned/that thene ony feoffement made by hym or ony other to his vse of ony of the premysses be voyde & of none effecte to exclude the kynge & his heyres or ony other for the warde & mariage/ of the heyre of ony of theym soo comyng in to this reame by the vertue of this acte .

¶ Anullyng of lettres patentes made to ony spirituell persone to be quytte for paymente of dysmes or for gaderyng of the same.

¶ Item the kynge our souereyn lord remembreth both as well his highnes as dyuers of his progenytours & predessessours kynges of englonde. haue made & graunted vpon feyned suggestyons to dyuers abbottes priours gardyns mapsters or rulers of other spirituell places & to their successours dyuers & many lettres patentes/ some of theym to be qupt & dyscharged of gadryng of dismes/ And some of theym to be qupt & dyscharged of payment of dysmes/ And some of theim to be qupt & discharged aswel of the gadring of dismes as of payment of dismes By the whiche eueri dis me whan someuer it be graunted/it is gretly mynyshed. and other places the more greuously charged wyth the gadring of the same / Remembreth also the grete charges that now ben in hande . and that the kepyng therof must aswell be to the relefe of thepm.that hath suche lettres patentes/as to other of his subgettes/ hath therfore ordeyned & enacted by auctorite of the sayd parliamente . that all the sayd lettres patentes/as for the premysses ben voyde/and of none effect By what someuer names thos persones to whom the lettres be made called or named/

¶ Anullyng of lettres patentes of ony offyce in the forest of Inglewode.

¶ Item for asmoche as thrugh the necligence of stuardes foresters & other kepers wythin the kyngis foreste of Ingle wood in the shire of Comberlond.and by mysusing of their offices.the dere & game is destroyed & goon bi occasion wher of/the sayd offyces requyren none actuell exercise. It is ther fore ordeyned & enacted by auctorite of this said parliament that all lettres patentes made by the kynge.our sayd souere yn lorde of ony office wythin the sayd forest be from the first day of this sayd parliament voyde & of none effect. Except

d iij

¶/Prouyded that it be ordeyned by the sayd auctorite that the
lettres patentes late made bi the kyng to thomas lord dacre
of thoffice of maister forster of the sayd forest stonde & be go
de & effectuel to the same thomas after the tenour & effect of
the same lettres patentes the sayd act notwythstondyng. ¶Pro
uyded also that this act extende not ne be preiudicpal to hen
ry erle of Northhumbr̄. of or for ony graūt lettres patentes
or confirmacōn made bi the kyng our souereyn lord to the sa
yd erle.   ¶That all lettres patentes made to
yomen of the corone . and gromes of the kyngis chambre/
for lacke of their attendaūce. be Boyd /

¶Item Where dyuerse yomen of the corone & gromes of þ
kyng our sayd souereyn lordis chambre/haue dyuers offy
ces & fees graūted to theim/bi his lettres patentes for the cō
sideracion of their attendaūce in the kyngis seruyce / Whiche
doo nor endeuour not theymself. in yeuyng their attendaūce
accordyng to their dutie/It is therfore ordeyned established &
enacted by thauctorite of the sayd parliamēt /that yf ony of
the sayd yomen or gromes doo nor yeue their attendaūce a
boute the kyngis highnes aacordyng to thordynaūce of his
chambre . that thēne all lettres patentes to theym or ony of
theym made or herafter to ony suche persone or persones to be
made. be of no better force ne effect but at þ kyngis plesure/

¶Item for asmoche as drapers & taylours/and other in
the cite of london & other places wythin this reame/that v
sen to selle wollen clothe at retapll by the yerdis/sellen a yer
de of clothe at excessiue price hauynge vnresonable lucre to
the grete hurte and enpouershyng of the kynges liege prple
byers of the same apenst equyte and good conscience. Wher
fore it is ordeyned by the kynge our souereyne lorde by thad
uyse of the lordes spirytuell and temporell/ and the comens

in this sayd parliamente assembled/ and by auctorite of the
same. that noo persone selle wythin this reame at retaplle/a
brode perce of wollen clothe of the fyneste makynge scarlet
grayned or other clothe grayned what colour soeuer it be to
ony of the kyngis subgettes aboue the price of xvj. shelin-
ges.a brode perce·And a brode perce of wollen cloth of ony
other colour oute of grayne. or ony maner russet of the fy-
nest not aboue the price of vj. shelinges vpon peyn to forfey
te for euery suche perce solde to ony the kyngis subgettes a-
boue the sayd price xl. shelinges/ And of euery other clothe
what colour sooeuer it be/ that is vnder the sayd price a bro
de perce to be solde to the kyngis subgettes after the rate of
the goodnes therof/And he that wyll sue for ony suche for
septure haue an actyon of dette therof aenst hym that soo
doth forfeite/In whiche action none essopy ne protection be
alowable/And the deffendaunt not to be admptted to wage his lawe/The kyng to haue theexecucion of the one halfe therof . and the partie that shall sue haue the other halfe/
This ordenaunce to begynne and take effecte from the feste of saynte Thomas the appostell/In the yere of our lorde
god.M.CCCC.lxxxix. And the same ordenaunce befo
re the same feest wythin the sayd cyte to be proclamed/

¶ Price of hattes & bonettes
¶ Item that where afore this tyme it hath be dayly vsed
and yet is/That certeyn craftemen named hatmakers and
capmakers don selle their hattes and cappes at suche an
outerageous price/ that where an hatte stondeth not theym
in xvj. pens they wylle selle it for iij. shelinges or xl. pens
And also a cappe that stondeth not theym in xvj. pens/they

wplle sell it for iiij shelinges. or B. shelinges.   And
by cause they knowe well that euery man muste occuppe
theym/they wplle selle theym at none eseat price. to the gret
te charge and domages of the kynges subgettes. and aga
ynst all good reason and conscyence   Wherfore it is ordi
ned enacted and stablisshed by the aduyse of the lordis spiri
tuell and temporell/and at the prayer of the coments in the
sayd parliamente assembled. and by auctorite of the same/
that noo hatter nor capper nor other persone selle not put to
selle ony hatte to ony of the kyngis subgettes aboue the pri
ce of xx.pens the beste/nor ony cappe aboue the price of ij she
linges Biij.pens the beste at the moost/   And for all hattes
z cappes vnder the value to be solde at suche a price as the
byer and seller may resonable agree/ Vpon peyne of forfey
ture for euery hatte or cappe otherwyse solde aboue the pry
ce abouesaid xl.shelinges/The one moyte therof to be to the
kynge our souereyne lorde/ and the other moyte to the par
tie that wpll sue and proue the sayd forfeyture by action or
by actions of det by wryt at the comen lawe/ by byll or pla
ynt after the custume of cyte or towne where it shall fortu
ne suche forfeyture to be. in the whiche like processe Juge
mente and execucion shall be had as is vsed in actions bil
les or pleyntes of det sued/after the cours of the comen law
or custume of towne or cyte afore sayd/And that the defen
daunte in ony suche action Bylles or pleyntes be not admpt
ted to woo his lawe.nor that ony protectyon or essoin therin
be alowed/This ordenaunce to begynne and take effect fro
the feest of saynt Thomas the appostle in the yere of our
&c.M.CCCC.Lxxxix/ And the same ordenauce before the
same feste wpthin the cite of london to be preclaymed/
    ¶ Of wyne z tolowse wooe

¶ Item that where grete mynysshyng and decaye hath be
now of late tyme of the naupe of this reame of Englond
and polenes of the mariners wythin the same / By the whi=
che this noble reame wythin short pwcesse of tyme wythout
reformacyon & had therin shall not be of habylite ne pow=
er to defende it selfe / Wherfore the kyng our souereyne lorde.
By thadupse of the lordis spirituell & temporell / and at the
praier of the comens in the said parliament assembled / and
By auctorite of the same / hath ordepned stablisshed & enacted
that no maner of persone of what degre or condpcyon that
he be / conuey nor brynge in to this sayd reame / Irlond wa=
les calays or the marches therof or berwyk / from the fest of
the Natiuyte of saynte Johñ the Baptist that shall be in the
pere of our lorde god. M. CCCC. lxxxx. ony maner wp=
nes of the growthynge of the duchie of Guyen or gascoyñ=
ne or wood called Tolowse woxe. But suche as shall be con=
ueyed anentred and brought in shyp or shippes. wherof our
sayd souerein lord or some of his subgettes of this reame
of englond Irlonx wales calays or berwpcke ben owners
possessours and proprietaries / And the mapster vnder god
and the marpners of the same shyppe or shippes Englisshe
irisshe or walshe or men of berwyshe or men of calays or of
the marches of the same for the more partie. Vpon pepne to
forfeyt the same wpnes and wood soo broughte contrary to
this act / the one half therof to the kyng / and other halfe to
him or theim that seasith the same wpne or woxe / And
also hath ordepned and stablisshed by the sayd auctorpte that
noo persone inhabpted wpthin this reame other than mar
chautes strauigers from the said fest of sapnt Johñ freight
ne charge wpthin this reame or wales ony shippe or other
vessel of ony allen or strauiger with ony maner marchadise

to be caryed oute of this reame or Wales/ or to be broughte
in to the same yf he maye haue sufficyente freighte in ship:
pes or Vesselles of the deynszens of this reame in the same
porte where he shall make his freighte/ Vpon payne to forfei
te the same marchaundyses. the one halfe therof to the kyn
ge our soueraygne lorde/ and the other halfe to hym or theym
whiche seaseth the same marchaundises/ ❡Prouyded
allwaye that this acte extende not to ony shyppe or shyppes.
hauyng ony of the said wares or marchaundyses constray
ned by tempest of weder or erimpes to arryue in ony porte
or place wythin this reame/ Soo that the owners of the
sayd wares and marchaudyses make therof noo sale with
in this reame other thenne for Vitaylle or repayryng of the
same shyppe or shyppes/ or takeling therof. whiche they of
necessitie be constrlled to make/

❡An acte Vpon byeng of wolles.

❡Item for the encrease and maynteynynge of drapery
and makynge of clothe wythin this londe/The kynge our
soueraygne lorde by the aduyse and assente of the lordes spiri
tuell and temporell/and the comens in this presente parli:
ament assembled/And by auctorite of the same hath ordey
ned establisshed and enacted/that noo maner of persone by
hym selfe/or by ony other bye or Bargeyn from the fyrst day
of marche/that shall be in the yere of our lorde.M.CCCC
lxxxix ony wolles thenne Vnshorne or take promyse of bar
geyne of ony wolles thenne Vnshorne of the growynge of
Berkshire oxenfordshire gloucestreshyre herefordeshire shrop
shire wurcestreshire Wiltesshire somersetshire dorsetshire hap
shire essex hertfordeshire cābrydge north.suff.kente surrey q

suffer / or ony of theym afore the feest of the Assumpcyon
of our lady thenne nexte ensuyng. or bye or bargeyne ony
wolles or take promyse of bargeyn of ony wolles that shal
growe in ony of the same shyres in ony yere or yeres to co
me after the said fest of Assumpcion of our lady ony tyme
before the same feste of assupcion of our lady that shall be
nexte after the sheryng of the same wolle or wolles / But
oonly suche persones as of the sayd wolles shall make or
doo to be made yerne or cloth wythin this reame. Upon peyn
of forfepture of the double value of all the wolles broughte
or to be bargeyned or taken by promyse of bargeyn contrary
to this ordenauce / Nor that ony marchaunt straunger by
hymself or by ony other persone in ony yere to come bye ony
wolles before the feest of the purifycacion of our lady nex
te after the clepppng or sheryng of the same Upon like peyn
of forfepture / The one halfe of suche forfepture to be had
to the kyngis Use. And the other halfe therof to the Use of
hym that wylle sue the partie that soo shall brake the sayd
ordenauce/And that ony persone that wyll sue in that par=
tie/haue an action of dette of the forsayd forfepture. and su
che processe in the same action to be had. as is in an acyon
of dette at the comen lawe/or after the custome of the.cyte bo
rugh or towne/Where it shall hap to be sued.And that noo
ensopn ne protection be alowed for the offendaut in that ac
tyon/ nor that the sayd offendaunt therin be admptted to
wage his lawe. It is also ordeyned by the sayd auc=
torite that noo maner persone keynge sworne to be a wolle
packer in ony wyse/after the sayd first daye of Marche/Bie
bargeyn ony maner wolle for ony suche marchaut straunger
wythin this reame Upon peyne of forfepture of the same
wolle soo boughte bargeyned, or gadred to the Use of

ony suche marchaunt straunger/ This ordenaunce to endure
from the sayd first daye of marche vnto thende & terme of x.
yeres thene next ensuyng.

¶ Actus sup pclam

¶ Item the kyng our souereyn lord considereth that by the
negligence mysdemeanyng fauour & other inordinat causes
of the iustices of peas in euery shire of this his reame / the
lawes & ordenaunces made for the politique wele peas & good
rule of the same. and for the profit suerte & restfull lyuyng
of his subgettes of the same be not duely executed accordin
ge to the tenour & effecte that they were made & ordeyned for.
Wherfore his subgettes ben greuously hurt/and out of sure
tie of their bodies & goodes to his grete dyspleysure/ for to
hym is noo thyng more ioyous thene to knowe his subget
tes to liue peasible vnder his lawes. and to encrease in wel
the & prosperite/ And to avoyde suche enormytees & iniuries
soo that his sayd subgettes maye liue restfull vnder his pe
as & lawer to their encreace/ He wyll that it be ordeyned & e
acted by thauctorite of this present parliamet that eueri iustice
of peas wythin eueri shire of this his sayd reame wythin
the shire where he is iustice of peas/do cause openly & solemp
ly to be proclaymed yerely/iiij. tymes in a yere. in iiij.pryn
cipall sessions the tenour of this proclamacyon to this byll
anneyed.And that euery iustyce of peas beyng present at o
ny of the sayd sessions yf they cause not the sayd proclamacy
on to be made in fourme aboue sayd/ shall forfeyte to our sa
id soueyn lord at euery tyme xx.shelinges

¶ De pclamacoe facienda.

¶ Henricus dei gra &c/ The kynge our souereyne lorde
considereth how dayly wythin this reame his coyne is tray
tourlsy counterfeyted murders robberyes felonyes ben

greuouſly coemmptted and woon. And alſo vnlawfull extẏ
uers poleneſſe vnlafull plẏpes extorſions mẏſdemenẏnges
of Shirweffes exchetours. and manẏ other enormẏtes & vn
lawful demenẏnges daily growẏth/ And more ſith within
this his reame to the grete dẏſplẏplſure of god hurt & enpo=
uerſhẏng of his ſubgettes/ and to the ſubuercion of the po=
lecie & good gouernaunce of this his reame/ For bẏ thẏſe
ſayd enormẏtees & mẏſchefes his pas is broken/ his ſub=
gettes troubled inquẏeted & impouerſhed. the houſbondrie of
this londe decaped/ Wherbẏ the chirche of englonde is vphol=
den/ the ſeruẏce of god contẏnued. euerẏ man therbẏ hathe
ſuſtenaunce euerẏ enheritour his rente for his londe/ For
repreſſhẏnge and auoẏdẏng of the ſayd mẏſchefes ſuffẏci=
ente lawes and ordenaunces ben made bẏ auctorẏte of ma=
nẏ and dẏuerſe parliamentes holden wẏthin this reame to
the grete coſte of the kẏng his lordis and comens of the ſa
me / And lackieth noo thẏnge/ But that the ſayd lawes ben
not put in due execucion. Whiche lawes ought to be put in
due execucion bẏ the Juſtice of peas in euerẏ ſhẏre of this
reame. to whom his grace hath put. and gẏuen full auctorẏ
te ſoo to do ſẏth the begẏnnẏng of his reigne. And now
it is comen to his knowlege that his ſubgettes be litell ea
ſed of the ſayd mẏſchefes bẏ the ſayd iuſtẏces. but bẏ manẏ
of thẏm rather hurte than helped. And if his ſubgettes có=
plaẏn to thiſe Juſtices of peas of onẏ wronges doon to the
ẏm/ they haue therbẏ noo remedẏ/ And the ſayd mẏſchefes
do encreaſe. and not ſubdued. And his grace conſidereth
that a grete part of the welth & proſperite of this londe ſtan
deth in that/ that his ſubgettes maẏ liue in ſuerte vnder his
peas in their bodies & goodes / And that the huſbondrẏ of
this londe maẏe encreaſe/ and be vpholden/ whẏche muſte

ſhall gyue hym a daie by his diſcreſcion to bzyng in his ſa
pd lettres or certifycat/And yf he fayle and bzyng not in at
ſuche a daye his ſapd lettres nor certifycat/thenne the ſame
perſone to loſe the benefyce of his clergy.as he ſhall wo that
is wythout ozders.

℩ Adnullyng of the ſeale of therlwome of Marche
℩ Item Where afore in the tyme of kyng edwarde the iiij
all feoffementes gyftes grauntes dvuerſe preſentementes
nompnacions releaces warrauntes ꝗ confirmacios made to
ony perſone or perſones of ony caſtelles honours manoyzs
londes ꝗ tenementes oz other heredptamentes or auaunta
ges percell or perteynyng to therlwome of marche. Oz pertey
nyng to ony maners londes oz tenementes/ and other here
dptamentes in demeſue.or reuerſion percell/ or perteynynge
to the ſapd erldom of marche were made ꝗ paſſed vnder a ſpe
ciall ſeale named the ſeale of the marches. Wherby is grow
en grete vexacion | trouble ꝗ dyſcepte of the ſubgettes of the
kyng our ſouereyne lorde. Wherfore it is enacted by thauc
torite of this preſent parliament/that all feoffementes gyf
tes grauntes dymiſes preſentementes nompnacyons/and
all other wzitynges.Wher to ſealing is requyſite to be made
After the feſt of the purifycacion of our lady in the v.yere
of the reygne of our ſouereyn lorde that now is.of ony par
cell of the ſapd erlewome he had done ꝗ made by the kyng our
ſapd ſouereyne lorde/vnder the brode ſeale of his chauncery
as it is vſed in all other thynges/concernynge the crowne/
by the cours of the comen lawe/and by none other ſeale.
℩ For the Mayre of London
℩ Item Where the maire of the cite of london for the tyme
beyng.is conſeruatour hauyng the conſeruacie of the water
and ryuer of thamps from the bzydge of Stanys vnto the

waters of pendale & mexwape/ It is soo that wythin fewe
yeres by tempeste of weder & grete habudance of waters in
the said ryuer of thamys. diuers Breckes issues & crekes ha
ue ben & growen oute of the sayd ryuer of thamys. And by
the same dyuers pastures medowes & groundes of dyuerse
persones ben drowned & ouerflowen/ In whiche Breckes issu
es & crekes & grounde drowned. the frie & Brode of fisshe for
the moost parte restith. and in the same places the sayd frie
& Brode in grete multitude ben dayly taken by the sayd fys=
shers there wyth vnlawfull engynes & nettes for bayte of
elis & coddys. And also for fedyng of their hogges to thut
ter destruction of the sayd frie & Brode/ wythout a remedy the
rather be prouyded/ The kyng our sayd souereyn lord by the
aduyse & assent of the lordes spirituell & temporell/and atte
the prayer of the sayd comens in the sayd parliament assem
bled.and by thauctorite of the same. hath ordeyned establis=
shed & enacted/ that the Mayre of London & his successours
maires for the tyme beyng haue the conseruacy & rule & like
auctorite in euery of the sayd Breckes issues & crekes & gro=
ude soo drowned.and ouer flowen as ferre as the water eb=
beth & flowyth as towchyng the punycyon for vsing of vn
lawfull nettis & other vnlawfull engynes in fysshyng li=
ke as he & his predecessours haue had or hath in the same
water & ryuer of thamys. wythin the bondes afore rehersed /
And to doo all other like correction & punysshemente there
concernyng the reformacion and redresse of vnlawfull net
tes & engines/as he & his predecessours haue vsed & owe to
vse in the sayd ryuer of thamys. le Roi le Vuelt/ ¶Pro=
uyded alway that the mayre of London nor his successours
maires for the tyme beyng/ haue not the conseruacion nor
rule ne auctorite in ony of the sayd Breckes issnes crekes &

groundes so drowned. and ouerflowen wythin the kyngis
grounde or keyng wythin ony frauchises of ony person or
persones spirytuell or temporell/ as touchyng the punyey:
on for vsing of vnlawfull nettes & other vnlawfull engy
nes in fysshyng nor to doo ony correction or punysshmēt the
re concernyng the reformacion & redresse of vnlawfull net:
tes & engynes / as the sayd mayre & his predecessours haue
vsed. and owe to vse in the sayd ryuer of Thamys

❡ The Ile de Wyght

❡ Item for asmoche as it is to the kyng our souereyn lor
de grete suerte/and also to the suerte of the reame of englon
de. that the Ile of Wyght in the countie of Sutht be well in
habited with englisshe peple for the defense aswell of his au
cien empes of the reame of fraunce/as of other parties! The
whiche ile is latly decaied of peple by rason that many tow
nes & vyllages ben lete downe. and the feldes dyked & made
pastures for bestes & catelles. And also many dwellyng
places fermes & fermeholders haue of late tyme be vsed to be
taken in to one mānys holde & handes/that of olde tyme we
re wonte to be in many seuerall persones holdes & handes/
and many seuerall housholders kept in thaym. And therby mo
che peple multiplied / and the same Ile therby well inhabited
the whiche now by thoccasion aforsayd is desolate / and not
inhabyted/but ocupyed wyth bestes & catelles. Soo that yf
hasty remedy be not prouyded. that ile can not be long kept
& defended/but open & redy to thandes of the kyngis empes/
whiche god forbede/ For remedie wherof it is ordeyned en:
acted & stablysshed by thaduyse & assent of the lordes spiritu:
ell & temporell. and the comens in this present parliamente
assembled/and by auctorite of the same. that fromhensforth
noo maner of person of what estate degree or condycion be

is or ſhall be) take ony ſeuerall fermes&moo thenne one. of
maners londes & tenemētes perſonages or tithes wythin the
ſaid ile. Wherof the ferme of thēm all togeder ſhall excede p̃
ſome of x.marke yerely/And yf ony ſeueral leſes afore this
tyme haue ben made/ to ony perſone or perſones of dyuerſe
ſundri fermeholdes ouer the ſaid yerely value of x.marke thē:
ne the perſone or perſones that now holde the ſaine. to cheſe
one or moo of the ſaid fermeholdes at his pleiſur/Soo that
the ferme of thepm all ſoo choſen be not aboue the yerely va:
lue of x.marke to holde after the fourme of his lees/and the
remnaut from the feſt of ſaynt myckell tharchangel whiche
ſhall be in the yere of our lorde M.CCCC.lxxxx.to ceaſe
& be vtterly voyde/And the ocupier & termer of thepm from
thens to be dyſcharged ayenſt his leſſour of the rente reſer:
ued vpon the ſame leeſes/And yf ony perſone doo here after
the contrare of this act/ that thene the leeſſe in that behalfe
forfeyt to the kyng for euery ſucke takyng x.li. Prouyded
allwayes that they whiche haue payed ony fynes or made o
ny byldyng or done grete reperacion vpon ony ſucke ferme
and be put from the ſayd ferme by reaſon of this act ſhal be
recompenſed for ſucke byldyng or reparacion/as riſt & good
conſciēce requyren/that recompence to be adiudged bi the diſ
crecion of the capitayne of the ſayd ile/for the tyme beynge
or his lieftenaut of the ſame in his abſence/

⸿ Wardes

⸿ Item where by an eſtatute made at markebridge/ It
was ordeyned p̃ whan tenautes made feoffemētes in frau:
de to make the lordes of the fee. to leſe their wardes/The lor
des ſkelde haue written to recouer their wardes ayenſt ſucke
feoffes as in the ſaid eſtatute amonge other thynges appe
reth more pleynly atte large/Syth the makynge of whiche

estatute many pmagynacions haue ben had ҁ yet ben vsed
aſwell by feoffementes fynes ҁ recoueres as otherwiſe/ to
put lordes from theyr wardes of londes holden of theym by
knyghtes ſeruyce · It is therfore ordeyned eſtabliſhed ҁ enac
ted by auctorite of the ſaid preſent parliamēt · that ҏ ſaid eſ
tatute of markeburgh be obſerued ҁ kept in al maner of thin
ges after the fourme ҁ effect therof /And ouer that it is or
deyned ҁ enacted bi the ſaid auctorite that yf ony perſone or
perſones of what eſtate degree or condicyon be or they be of
or were after ſhall be/ſeyſed in demeane or in reuerſion of eſ
tate of heritauce beyng tenaut immediat to the lordis of ony
caſtelles maners londes ҁ tenemētes or other herediiamen
tes holden by knyghtes ſeruyce · in his or their demeane/ as
of fee · to thuſe of ony other perſone or perſones ҁ of his hey
res onely · be to whos vſe · he or they be ſo ſeiſed dieth his hey
re beyng wythin age / noo wylle by hym declared nor made
in his lif · touchyng the prēmyſſes or ony of theym /The lor
de of whom ſuche caſtelles maners londes tenementes ҁ he
redytamētes ben holden immediatly ſhal haue a writ of riȝt
of warde aſwell for body as for the londe/as the lord ſholde
haue had yf the ſame auceſtre had be in poſſeſſion of that eſ
tate · ſoo beyng in vſe at tyme of his deth · ҁ noo ſuche ſtate
to his vſe made /And yf ony ſuche heire be of full age · at ҏ
deth of his auceſtre to pay a relief as his auceſtre whos hey
re he is had be in poſſeſſion of that eſtate ſoo beyng in vſe
at tyme of his deth/ and no ſuche eſtate to his vſe made nor
had · It is alſo ſtabliſhed ҁ enacted by the ſaid auctorite · that
ſuche heire or heyres ſo beyng in warde ſhal haue like action
of waſt apēſt the ſaid lordis or apenſt theym in whos war
de they ſo be as they or ony of theym ſhold haue had/ and re
couere ſuche domages ҁ ſuche penalties to be to the ſaid lord

and gardeyns as sholde haue ben if their auncestres had dir
ed therof. seised/ And ouer yf ony suche lorde beyng ony su
che wryt of right of warde apenst suche persone or persones
and be barred in the same that thenne the same deffendaunt
or defendauntes shall recouer damages apenst the sayd plein
tifs for their wrongfull vexacion in the same/ Prouyded
alwayes that this acte/ begyn to take effecte of theyres of
theym that shal dye after the fest of Ester that shall be in
the yere of our lord M.CCCC.lxxxx.

℣ Forgynge & coūtrefeytyng of golde & siluer of other
londes suffred to renne in this reame is made treyson/

℣ Item for asmoche as by the kyngis sufferaūce/ dy
uers coigne of golde & siluer. whiche be not of the kingis pro
per coygne of englonde be currante in payment wythin this
reame dyuers & many euyll disposed persones percepuyng y
the forgyng & coūtrefeytyng of suche coygnes is nether felo
ny nor treyson/ presume & take vpon theym for their syngu
ler auayle & profyte to coūtrefeyt & forge suche coynes/to the
grete hurte & preiudyce/aswell of the kyng our souereyn lor
de as to the hurte of all the kyngis subgettes It is therfo
re ordeyned & stablished by auctorite of the sayd parliament
that the coūtrefeytyng & forgyng of euer suche coyne/ be ad
iuged treyson, as it is of the coūtrefeytyng of the propre coi
ne of the kyng of this reame/

℣ For kepyng vp of houses for husbondrye
℣ Item the kynge our souereyn lorde hauynge a singuler
pleysur aboue all thynge to auoyde suche enormytees & mys
cheuious, as ben hurtful & preiudyciall to the comen wele of
this his londe and his subgettes of the same/ Remembreth
that amonge all other thynges grete incouenyences/dayly
doo encrease by desolacion and pullyng downe and wylfull

                      d   iij

waſt of houſes and townes wpthin this his reame/and le
png to paſture londes whiche cuſtumably haue ken Vſed in
tplthe. Wherby poleneſſe is growñe and kegynnyng of all mpſ
cheuous dayly dooth encreaſe/ffor where in ſome townes ij
hundred perſones were occupped & liued by their lawfull
labours. now ken there occupped ij. or iij. herdemen/ and the
reſidue falle in polenes/the huſbondrie whiche is one of the
greteſt comoditees of this reame is gretly decaped/churches
deſtroped / the ſerupſe of god wpthdrawen/ the bodies there
keried not praied for/The patrone & curates wronged. the de
fenſe of this londe apenſt our enmyes outwarde febled and
impeyred/to the grete diſplepſur of god. to the ſubuerſion of
the policie & good rule of this londe/and remedy be not ther
fore haſtly purueped/Wherfore the kyng our ſapd ſouerein
lorde. by thaduyſe of the lordes ſpirituell & temporel/and the
comens in the ſapd parliament aſſembled. and by auctorite
of the ſame hath ordeyned enacted & ſtabliſhed that noo per
ſone what eſtate degree or condicyon that he ke/that hath or
np hous or houſes that at onp tyme within iij. peres paſſed
hath ken or that now is or hereafter ſhal ke/ leten for ferme
wpth xx. acres of londe at leeſt or more/lipnge in tpllage &
huſbondrie/that the owner or owners of eueri ſuche houſe
or houſes & londe. ke bounde to kepe ſuſtepn & mayntene hou
ſes & bploynges upon the ſapd growñde & londe conuenpent
& neceſſarie for mayntenyng & upholdyng of the ſapd tpllage & huſbondrie/ And pf onp ſuche owner or owners of o-
np ſuche houſe or houſes & londe take kepe & occuppe onp ſu
che hous or houſes & londe in his or their owne handes that
the ſapd owner or owners by the ſapd auctorite ke bounde/
in like wpſe to kepe & mayntene houſes & bploynges upon p
ſapd growñde & londe conuenpent & neceſſary for p mayntening

& vpholdyng of the sayd tillage & husbondrie / And yf ony
man doo contrarie to the premysses or ony of theim. that
thenne it be liefull to the kyng/ yf ony suche londes or hou:
ses be holden of hym. immedyatly/ or to the lordes of the fees
yf ony suche londes ben holden of hepm/ immediatly to rescei
ue yerely halfe the balue of thyssues & profytes of ony su:
che londes. wherof the house or hou:ses ben not soo mayntened
& sustepned / And the same halfendele of thissue & profytes
to haue holde & kepe to his or their owen bse/wythoute ony
thyng therfore to be payed or peuen. to suche tyme as the sa
me house or houses be suffycyently bplded or repayred ayen
And that noo maner of freholde be in the kyngne in ony su
che lord or lordes by the takyng of ony suche profytes of or
in ony suche londes in noo maner of fourme but oonly the
kyng/And the sayd lord or lordes haue power to take recei
ue & haue the sayd pssues & profytes as is aboue sayd/And
therfore the kyng. or the sayd lord or lordes to haue power
to dystreyne for the same/ issues & profytes to be had & percep
ued by thepm/ in fourme aboue sayd by auctorite of this pre
sente acte/

¶ Actions populers

¶ Item that where actions populers in dyverse causes ha
ue ben ordeyned bi many good actes & statutes afore this ti
me made for the reformacion of extorsious mayntenaūce op
pressions Iniuries exactions & wronges bsed & comytted
wythin this reame/ whiche actions ben berey penall to alle
mysdoers & offenders in suche actions condempned and mo
che profitable/ as well to the kyng as to euery of his subget:
tes. that thepm wyll sue & mayntene yf the same actions so
sued & comenced myght be truly pursued wythoute coupy or
collusion. But now is so comenly bsed within this reame

c   iiij

that if ony suche offeder offendyng in causes Where ony of
the sayd actyons lie/than the sayd myssoers or offenders in
eschewyng to lese the said penaltes wyll cause an action po=
puler to be comenced apenst theym/By couyn of the pleyntif
Bpon that case. Wherin they haue soo offended/Or elles yf o
ny suche action populer be comenced apenst ony suche sayd
offender by gode feyth. than the same offender wyll delay the
sayd action other by none apperaunce. or by trauerse. and han
gyng the same action the same offender wyll cause like ac
tion populer to be brought apenst hym bi couyn for the same
cause a offence. that the first action was sued/And than bi
couyn of the pleyntyf. in that ij. action he wyll be condemned
other bi confession feyned/triel or relese/Whiche condempnaci
on or relese so had by collusion a couyn pleted by the said of
fender shall barre the pleyntyf. in the action sued in gode fe=
yth/and by thise subtyl meanes of collusion a couyn the sa=
id good actes a statutes full seldom ben executed apenst su=
che offenders/Whiche causeth theim to be bolder to offende the
kyng/as wel in brekyng of the sayd statutes lawes a peas.
as in robbyng murdryng exactios takyng quarelles mai=
tenyng and the kyngis pour subgettes by extorcion a ma=
ny other Bnlawful meanes oppressyng/Therfore the kyng
our sayd souereyne lord in refourmyng of the premysses bi
thaduyce a assent of the lordys spirituell a temporell/ and
at the request of the said comens in this said presente par=
liament assembled a by auctorite of the same hath ordeyned
stablished a enacted/that if ony persone or persones hereafter
sue wyth good feyth ony action populer/and the deffendaut
or defendautes in the same action plede ony maner of recoue
re of action populer in barre of the sayd action/or elles that
the same defendaut or defendautes plede that he or they before

that tyme barred ony suche pleyntif oz playntifes in ony su
che action populer/that thêne the playntyf or pleyntifes in p̃
action taken wyth good feyth may abarre that the said reco
uere in the sayd action populer was had by coupn/or elles
to abarre that the sayd playntif or playntifes was oz were
barred in the sayd action populer by coupn/ that than yf af=
terwarde the sayd collusion or coupn soo abarred be lawful=
ly founden/the pleyntif or pleyntifes in that action sued with
good feyth shall haue recouere accordyng to the nature/ of
the action and execucion vpon the same/In likewyse & effec
te as though noo suche afore had be had/ And ouer that
it is enacted & ordeined by thauctorite aforsaid/ that in eue
ry suche action populer wherin the defendaunt or defendaun
tes shal be lawfuly condempned or attepned of coupn or col
lusion as is aforsayd/ that euery of the same defendauntes
haue enprisonement of ij. yere by pcoesse of capias and be
lagaed to be sued wythin the yere after suche iugemente had
Or at ony tyme after tyll the sayd defendaunt oz defendau=
tes be had & enprisoned as is aforsayd/ And that aswel at
the kyngis sute/as of euery other that wylle sue in that be=
halfe. And that noo relecase of ony comen persone here after
to be made.to ony suche partie wheder before or after ony ac
tion populer oz endytment of the same had oz comenced or
made haueyng the same action be in ony wyse auaylable/ or
effectuel to let or to surcease the sayd action endytement pro=
cesse or execucion . Prouyded allway that noo playntif or
playntyfes be in ony wise excepued to abarre ony coupñ in o
ny action populer where the poynt of the same action oz el
les that coupñ or collusioñ haue bin ones tried or lawfully
founde.wyth the pleyntif or pleyntifes or ayenst theim.by try
all of rij meñ/and not otherwyse/

        d B

¶ Item for kepyng of frye of fysshe of
the see in Orforde hauen/

¶ Item where dyuers statutes & ordenaūces for saupnge
& kepngy of frie & brode of fysshe in fresshe ryuers of this rea
me before this time haue ben made & ordepned.But for sauin
ge & kepyng of frie & brode of fysshe resortyng out of the see
and saltwaters in to hauens & crekes wythin the sayd re;
me/onp ordenaunce generall hath not be purueyed ne made
how be it hit were full requysite and profytable to al the co
mens of this reame/and specialy to the kyngis subgettes &
inhabptantes nygh adiunpng to the Masse & hauen of Or
forde in the coūtie of suffolke/wythin whiche nasse & hauen
there is yerely grete multptude of spawone & brode of all ma
ner fysshes of the see/ And there wolde largely encrease &
multpplie. yf they mpght there conuenyent tyme. be suffred
to abyde/But now it is soo that in late dayes for a singu;
ler couetise & lucre in takyng of a fewe grete fysshes certeyn
persones haue vsed to set & ordepne/certepn botes called stall
botes festened wyth anctes hauyng wyth thepm suche ma;
ner vnresonable nettes & engpnes/that almaner frie & bro;
de of fysshe in the sayd hauen multeplied is taken & distroy;
ed.as well grete fysshes vnresonable as the sayd frye & brode
to nombre innumerable. Wyth the whiche frie & brode the
sayd persones wyth parte therof fede their hogges/and the re
sidue they put & lep it in grete pyttes into the grounde/Why;
che elles wolde torne to suche perlous infection of eyr that
noo persone thider resortpnge sholde it abyde or suffre.to the
grete hurt of the kyngis liege peple wythin this reame/and
specially to the kyngis subgettes and inhabptantes wyth;
in the shire of Norfolke & Suffolke/And also causeth gre
te scarsite of fysshe in that countrees. Where afore this tyme

was wounte to be grete plente. Wherfore the kyng our sa=
yd souerayne lord of his noble grace. By the aduyce & assent
of the lordis spirituell & temporell/ and at the prayer of the
sayd comens in the sayd parliamente assembled/ and by auc
torite of the same/ hathe ordeyned stablisshed & enacted/ that
all suche stalle botes nettes & engynes aforsayd from the fir
ste daye of Aprill. that shall be in the yere of our lord. M.
CCCC.lxxxp. be not occupied nor vsed for the destroyeng
or takynge of ony frye or brode of fysshe/ wythin the hauen
aforsayd vpon peyn of forfeyture of y ki. at euery tyme that
ony persone/ shall happen to do contrarie to this ordenaunce.
thone halfe therof to be to the kyng/ And the other halfe to
hym/ that shal happen to fynde the same forfeyture/ and she=
we the same by informacion in to the kyngis eschequer/ the
re to be determyned after the cours of the same courte/ And
ouer that it is ordeyned by the auctorite aforsayd that the
Justices of peas of the shires of Norffolke & Suffolke.
for the tyme beyng haue auctorite & power to enquere in the
ir seuerall sessions of al the botes nettes & engynes vsed or
occupied contrary to this ordenaunce aforsayd/ And the of
fenders therin before theym presented to punysshe. as by their
discrescion shall be thoughte lawfull & resonable/ This ac
te and ordenauce to endure vnto the begynnyng of the nex
te parliamente /

¶ A bylle atte the sute of Brouwerers
¶ Item in the sayd parliamet it was shewed vnto the kin
ge our souerayn lorde bi the wardeyn & felisship of Brouwerers
in the cite of london and of euery other cytie towne & place
of this reame / That were thorough mynysshynge of the

weight of Venyce florence and Jeane golde and the vntrue
packyng therof aswel the sayd browderis as other the kyn
gis subgettes byers of browded werkes wythin this reame
susteyn & bere grete los hinderaunce & dysauautage. for where
in tymes past the poude weyght of golde of ony of the sayd
coutrees of Benyce florence & Jeane was woute to kepe the
full weyght of xij. Vnces/and thene comenly solde at xxviij.
shelinges iiij d. or ther aboute/the golde packed whiche they
now selle for a poude weight weyeth not aboue Vij. Vnces &
solde for in.li sterling the packe/ And also the bryngers in
to this reame of the sayd golde soo descrpuable & vntruly pac
ken the said golde that the threde & colour vnder the first shelb
is gretter & courser thene is shewed in sight & not accordyng
to the outwarde shelbe. to thutter enpouershyng of the sayd
browderis and also grete charge & disauautage of the byers
of browded werke as is aforsaid Wherfore the kyng our sa
yd souerayne lord by the aduyce and assente of the lordys
& the comens in this present parliamet assebled/and by auc
torite of the same/ hath ordeyned establisshed & enacted that
noo persone what degre or condycion he be from the fest of es
ter that shall be in the pere of our lord M.CCCC.lxxxx.
bryng & put to sale wythin this sayd reame ony golde of Be
nyce florence or Jeane/as or for a poude weyght/but yf the
same golde soo put or offred to sale for a poude weight/con
teyn in the weight fully xij Vnces And also that the same
golde so packed be in gretnes of threde & colour wrought ac
cordyng to the outwarde shelbe. werof vpon peyn of forfeitu
re of the said gold solde or put to sale for a poude weight not
beeing fully xij Vnses or not wrought in gretnes of threde
in colour accordyng to the outwarde shelbe. or elles the Value
therof/thone half of the said forfeiture to be to the kyng our

foueraypn lord/and thother halfe to hym or thepm of his sub=
gettes that shal seafe ʒ proue the fame forfaitures by actioõ
of det at the comen lawe/or by byll or playnt.after the cuftu=
me of cite or towne wher shall fortune ony fuche forfaytu
res to fall ʒ be/Jn whiche actions the defendaut shall not be
admytted to do his lawe/nor ony effoyn ne protection shal
be for fuche defendaut alowed.Prouyded that this act afore
the fayd feft of Efter within the cite of london be proclamed
this act ʒ ordenauce to endure vnto y̌ beginyng of the next
parliament.   ❡ Caryeng of golde ʒ filuer ouer the fee
❡ Jtem where in a parliamēt begon ʒ holden at weftmyn
fter the xvj day of Januarij in the xvij.yere of kyng edwar
de the iiij.amonge other it was ordeyned by auctorite of the
fame parliamēt/that noo pfone shold carie ne make to be ca
ried out of this reame or wales from noo part of the fame o
ny maner of money of the coygne of this reame nor money
of the coygne of other reames londes or lordships nor plate
veffel maffe Bullion nor iuelles of golde garneffhed or vn=
garnpfhed or of filuer without the kyngis licence. But fuche
perfones as ben dispenfed wythin the ftatute made in the ij.
yere of the reygne/of the kyngis Bleffed vncle kyng henri the
vij.and other diuers ftatutes made vpon xpn of felonye.
ʒ to be demed ʒ reputed as a felon/the fame felonie to be herd
ʒ determyned in like maner ʒ fourme ʒ afore fuche perfones
as other felonyes vfuelly were herd ʒ determyned wythin
this reame/as in the faid ftatute more pleinli doeth apere.the
whiche ftatute ʒ ordenauce was made to endure from the fef
of Efter in the xviij.yere of the reygne of the fayd kyn=
ge Edwarde the fourth vnto the ende of feuen yeres thene
next enfuyng fithen the whiche vij.yeres exfpired/the gold
ʒ filuer of the coigne of this reame hath ʒ daily is ʒ ben ca=

ries & coueyed in to flaudres normandie Bretapne Burdeaux
prlondx. and other parties beyonde the see/ aswel by marcha
unt strangers as by denisens/to the grete enpouershynge
of al this reame/ and gretter is like to be wythout remedie
therfore hastly be prouyded. The kyng our souerepne lorde þ
prempsses considered by thadupse of the lordes spirituell &
temporell. and at the prayer of the comens in this presente
parliament assembled/and by auctorite of the same hath or
depned stablisshed & enacted. that the sayd statute made in the
sayd xviij. pere of kyng edwarde the iiij. be & stonde a statu;
te good & effectuel with all the prempsses in the same/and
be obserued kept & put in due execucion from the fest of the
purifycacion of our lady that shall be in the pere of our lor
de god M.CCCC.lxxxix. and to endure unto the ende of
xv. pere nepte supng/ And ouer that by the same auctorite
it is ordepned & enacted that noo persone dwellyng or inha
bityng wythin this reame from the sayd fest of purifycaci;
on pape or deliuer wyttynglp by wap of exchauge or other;
wyse to onp marchaut or other persone stranger borne oute
of the kyngis obepsaunce for onp marchaudise or wares or
in onp otherwpse onp maner peces of golde copnned in this
reame or in onp other reame or onp plate Bessel masse bul
lion ne Juelp of golde wrought or unwrought vpon payn
to forfepte & lose the double some or double value of al suche
money of golde copnned plate Bessell masse bullion or Juel
of golde or siluer payed deliuered or eschauged contrarie to
this acte/ The one halfe of the same forfepture to be to the
kpnge or souerepne lorde/and the other halfe to onp of his
subgettes that wplle sease it or sue for onp suche paymente
deliuerauce of eschauge made or to be made cotrarie to this
act/and þ it be leful to þ kingis subgettes in this cause to
                                                        sue

for the sayd forfeyture by action of dette by writte at the co
men law by bylle or playnt after the custume of ẏ cite por
te or towne where it shall happen ony forfeyture to falle/ &
&/or by Informacyon to be made in the kyngis eschequer
And that noo protection nor essoine be alowable in ony su
che action or informacyon/

℟ Item where it is ordeyned in the tyme of kyng Edwar
de the first by the statute de finibz that notes & fynes to be le
uyed in the kyngis court afore his iustices sholde be openly
& solempny rede. And that plees in the meane tyme sholde
cease. And this to be done by two dayes in the weke/after
the descrecion of the Justyces. as in the same statute more
pleynly apereth/The kyng our sayd souereyn lorde consid̃e
reth that fynes ought to be of the grettest strength to aboy
de stryues & debates and to be fynall ende & conclusion and
of suche effect were take afore a statute made of none clay
me/and now is vsed the contrary to the vnyuersall trouble
of all the kyngis subgettes. Wylle therfore it be ordeyned
by the aduyse of the lordis spirituell & temporell and the co
mens in the sayd parliament assembled/ and by auctoryte
of the same/that after the ingrosing of euery fyne to be leuy
ed. after the fest of Ester that shall be in the yere of our lord
M.CCCC.lxxxx.in the kyngis courte afore his Justices
of the comen place/of ony londes tenementes or other heredy
tamentes the same fyne be openly and solempny rede & pro/
claymed in the same courte the same terme/and in iij. termes
thenne next folowyng/ the same ingrosyng/in the same cour
te/atte iiij. seuerall dayes in euery terme/And in the same
tyme that it is soo rod & proclaymed all plees ceasses and
the sayd proclamacions soo had and made / the sayd fyne to

&c fynall ende and conclude as well pryuees as estraugers
to the same . Excepte wymmen couert other than ben parti
es to the sayd fyne   .And euery persone thenne being
wythin age of xxj. yeres/in pryson or oute of this reame.
or not of hole mynde/at the tyme of the sayd fyne leuyed not
parties to suche fyne.And sauyng to eueri persone or perso
nes & to their heires other thêne the parties in ỹ said fyne su
che right clayme & interest. as thei haue to or in the sayd londes
tenementes or other heredytamentes. tyme of suche fyne in
growsed. Soo that they pursue their title claym or interesse. By
way of action or lawfull entre wythin .v.yeres next after
the sayd pclamacions had & made.And also sauyng to al o
ther persones suche action right title clayme & interesse in or
to the sayd londes tenementes or other inheredytamentes as
first shall growe/remayn or descende or come to thepm after
the said fyne engrowed & pclamacion made/Bi force of ony
yefte in the taylle/or by ony other cause or mater had & made
&fore the sayd fyne leuyed. Soo that they take their action
or pursue their sayd right & tytle accordyng to the law/ with
in .v.yeres nexte after suche action right tytle/clayme or in
teresse to thepm accrued descended remayned fallen or come/
And that the sayd persones & their heyres may haue their sa
yd action ayest the pernour of thepfytes of the said londes &
tenementes & other heredytamentes tyme of the sayd action
to be taken/And yf the same persones at tyme of suche acty
on right & title accrued descended remained or come vnto the
pm by couert de Baron or wythin age.in prisone or oute of
this londe or not of hole mynde . That thêne it is ordeyned
By the sayd auctorite that their action right and title to be re
serued and saued to thepm and to their heyres vnto the tyme
they come and be at thepr full age/of xxj.yeres out of prison
wythin

this londe ßncouert ꝗ of hole mynde/Soo that they or thepr
heyres take their said actions or their lawfull entre ac=
cordynge their right ꝗ title wythin .ß. peres nexte after that
they come ꝗ ße at their full age oute of prison wythin this
londe ßncouert ꝗ of hole mynde/ And the same actions put
sue or other lawfull entre take/accordyng to the law/ And
also it is ordeyned by thauctorite aforsayd that all suche per
sones as ße couert de Baron not partie to the fyne/and euery
persone ßeynge wythin age of xxj. peres in prison or oute of
this londe or not of hole mynde/at tyme of the sayd fynes ße
uped ꝗ engroced/and by this sayd act afore except hauyng o
ny right or title or cause of action. to ony of the sayd londes
ꝗ other enhabitamentes that they or their heyres inheritable
to the same/take their sayd actions or lawfull entre accor
dyng to their right ꝗ title wythin .ß. peres nexte after they co
me ꝗ ße of ful age/of xxj. peres out of prison ßncouert with
in this londe and of hole mynde/ and the same actpons sue/
or their lawfull entre take.ꝗ pursue accordyng to the lawe
And yf they woo ꝗ take not their actions ꝗ entre.as is afor
sayd that they ꝗ eueri of thepm ꝗ their heires/and the heires
of euery of thepm ße concluded by the said fynes for euer in
like fourme/as they ßen that ße parties or pryuees to the sa=
pd fynes. Sauynge to euery persone ꝗ persones not partpe
nor pryue/to the sayd fyne/their excepcion to auopde the sa=
me fyne/ßi that. that thos that were parties to the fyne/nor
ony of theim nor noo persone nor persones to their ße/ne to
the ße of ony of thepm/had noo thynge in the londes ꝗ te=
nementes comprysed in the sayd fyne at the tyme of the sa=
pd fyne ßuped/ And it is ordeyned ßi the sayd auctorite that
euery fyne that hereafter shal ße ßuped in ony of the kpngis
courtes of ony maners londes tenementes ꝗ other possessions

after the maner vse and fourme. that fynes haue ben leuied
afore the makyng of this acte. be of like force effecte τ auc
torite/ as fynes soo leuyed be or were afore the makyng /of
this acte. this act or ony other acte. in this said parliament
made or to be made. not wythstondyng. And that euery persone be at his liberte. to leuye ony fyne. herafter/ after his
pleysure/ Wheder he wylle after the fourme contepned τ ordei
ned in and By this acte/or after the maner τ fourme afore ti
me vsed/

ANNOTATIONS.

———◦◦❂◦◦———

fol. 1 recto, line 11.

Fermedowne. 1 Hen. VII. c. 1, Rot. Parl. nu. 66. Formedon was a writ at common law by which an heir to lands or
tenements by virtue of an entail claimed his right to recover.
" The word is derived from forma donationis, so called
because the gift doth comprehend the form of the gift : there
be three kinds of formedon, viz : the first is the descender
to be brought by the issue intail, which claim by descent
per formam doni. The second is the Reverter which lieth
for him in the Reversion, or his heires or assignes, after the
estate tail be spent. The third is the Remainder which the
law giveth to him in the remainder his heires or assignes
after the determination of the estate tail : all which you
may reade in the Register and F N B " (Fitzherbert's
Natura Brevium) *Coke on Litt :* ed : *Hargrave.*

fol. 1 recto, line 24.

Pernours of the profytes, Pernours, from the French
preneurs from the verb prendre, takers of the profits.

fol. 1 recto, line 28.

Vourchers is when a *præcipe quod reddat* of land is
brought against a man, and another ought to warrant the
land again to the tenant, then the tenant shall *vouch* him
to warranty. Voucher also is the calling in of some person
to answer the action that hath warranted the title to the
tenant or defendant.

fol. 1 recto, line 28.

Eide pyer, an error in Caxton's print for pryer. "In real actions the tenant may pray in aid, or call for the assistance of another, to help him to plead, because of the feebleness or imbecility of his own Estate: thus a tenant for life may pray in aid of him that hath the inheritance in remainder or reversion :— . . . . that is that he shall be joined in the action, and help to defend the title." *Bl: Com: B. III. p.* 300.

fol. 1 verso, line 15. (1 Hen. VII. c. 2, Rot. Parl. nu. 69.)

fol. 2 recto, line 15. (1 Hen. VII. c. 3, Rot. Parl. nu. 68.)

fol. 2 recto, line 22. *Merchauntes of the Staple.* In early times the revenues of the Crown were principally derived from impost duties on the exportation of commodities produced in this country. The word Staple in the sense of this enactment signifies fixed : Ducange derives Etape, the corresponding word in French at his date, from the old French word Estaple "nunc Etape" Nat : Bailey derives it from Stapel, *Dan.* ; Stapul, *Sax.* ; Stapel *Dutch and German.* Ducange explains it as "Emporium forum publicum, in civitatibus præsertim maritimis constitutum ubi merces extraneæ publice distrahuntur." Bailey says it signifies a public town where are store houses for commodities, also a city or town where Merchants jointly lay up their commodities for the better vending them by wholesale. Webster defines it as that which is fixed, or a fixed place : *the Merchants of the Staple* were first incorporated by Edw. III., in whose time they had their staple of wool at Calais : the chief staple commodity of England was for a long period its Wool, which was in great request amongst the Manufacturers of France and Flanders : "the Merchants of the Staple" says Anderson in his *Historical Deduction of the History of Commerce,* "were the first and ancientest Commercial Society in England, so named from their exporting the Staple wares of the kingdom : it was put under sundry regulations, and was the means of bringing in considerable

wealth, as well before as after the making of woollen cloths
here : they were privileged by many succeeding kings:
Henry III., Edw. II., Richard II., Hy. IV., and Henry V.,"
they bought the wool from the producers, and being
established in some certain place for its sale were termed
Staplers : the Netherlands being unable to grow sufficient
for their manufactures, took large quantities. The Staplers
in the 12th century collected the wool at some sea port
convenient for exportation, where they paid the king's duty.
In the year 1660 an Act was passed prohibiting the exportation of Wool, and soon afterwards the Wool Staplers
Company virtually became obsolete, having for many years
engrossed the foreign trade of England.

(1 Hen. VII. c. 4, Rot. Parl. nu. 67.)   .   fol. 2 verso, line 1.

Ordynaries, properly the Bishop of the Diocese himself,   fol. 2 verso, line 9.
but the term is used for every commissary, deputy, or
official of the Bishop or other judge ecclesiastical who has
judicial authority within the jurisdiction.

Aduoutre, adultery.   .   fol. 2 verso, line 14.

Henry the Seventh, error in Caxton for Henry the Sixth.   fol. 3 recto, l. 5 & 19.

Vj. shelinges viij. pens. The prevalence of this sum in   fol. 3 recto, line 9.
legal matters, such as fees, fines, etc., arises from the fact of
its being half a mark ; the mark being one of the oldest
coins of this realm, the value of which was 13s. 4d.

To hym that fyndeth it and proueth it, etc. This was   fol. 3 verso, line 1.
called suing by *action populer*, a very common procedure in
those times.   .

Shepes skynnes. In 1303 a complaint was made to Sir   fol. 3 verso, line 26.
John le Blount, Mayor of London, and the other civic
authorities, by " many good folks," cordwainers of the City,
that certain persons of their craft were in the habit of
unlawfully mixing the leather used in their workmanship,
basil or *sheepskin*, for example, with cordwain, and calf-

leather with cow-leather, and of making shoes of these
inferior kinds of leather and selling the same "to the
knights and other great lords of the land " for cordwain
and for kid. Sheepskins were almost exclusively used for
the manufacture of gloves.

fol. 4 recto, line 3. (1 Hen. VII. c. 6, Rot. Parl. nu. 72).

fol. 4 recto, line 3. *Fro beyonde the see,* i.e., from Brittany, where Henry had
resided from 1471 up to the time when he took the field
against Richard III.

fol. 4 recto, line 12. In *seintwarie or in hedyll,* in sanctuary or in hiding-
places ; hidel is interpreted by Bailey as signifying a
sanctuary or place of protection.

fol. 4 verso, line 7. *Dyssīn,* disseisina, unlawfully dispossessing a man of his
lands. " Disseis is a putting a man out of seizin, of ancient
time a disseisin was defined thus 'disseisin est un personel
trespasse de tortious ousterdel seizen.' " *Litt.*

fol. 4 verso, line 18. *Thomas and Elizabeth Wyndesore.* Thomas Windsor, of
Hanwell, Middlesex, married Elizabeth, eldest daughter
and co-heir of John Andrews, of Baylham, County Suffolk ;
he was an ancestor of the first line of the Earls of Windsor,
(not of the present, whose paternal name is Hickman.)
Thomas died in 1485, and was buried in Hanwell Church,
" where," says Lodge, in 1779, " is yet remaining under a
cornice a raised tomb on which were the figures of a gentleman and his lady, inlaid in brass, with an escutcheon of
their arms, but are now torn off, as also the inscription."

fol. 4 verso, line 17. *Sir John Coket prest, i.e.,* priest. Fuller in his Church
History of Britain, book VI., p. 352, ed. 1655, writes "More
Sirs than Knights." "Such Priests as have the addition of Sir
before their Christian names were men not graduated in the
University, being in *Orders,* but not in degrees." In the life
of Bishop Waynflete it is however said to have been a title
given to such as had taken a degree, and the case is adduced

by Dr. Chandler, of the Bishop's brother John, who was styled Sir, "perhaps as being B. A." In the buttery-books of St. John's Coll., Oxon, every Bachelor has the prefix of Sir,

(1 Hen. VII. c. 7, Rot. Parl. nu. 74.)

fol. 4 recto, line 1.

Bayle, bayliff, the bayliff errant appointed by the sheriff of the county to execute writs, summon the sessions, assizes, etc.

fol. 5 recto, line 6.

Rescusse, or Rescous in Law "is when the Lord distraineth in the land holden of him for his rent behind, if the distresse be rescued from him, &c." *Coke Litt.,* ed.: *Hargrave.* Here, however Rescusse simply means to rescue in the ordinary sense.

fol. 5 verso, line 28.

(1 Hen. VII. c. 8, Rot. Parl. nu. 70.) *Navee.* This term here merely implies the merchant navy; there was no royal navy at that period, and, whenever ships of war were wanted, vessels of the merchant service were armed and manned. The first ship of the royal navy was the Great Harry, built by Henry VII. at a cost of £14,000, the same amount as he is said to have expended in the erection of his chapel at Westminster Abbey. (Stow, by Howes, p. 484.)

fol. 6 recto. line 11.

Guyen and Gascoygne, i.e., Bordeaux wines. See also Statute 4 Hen. VII. c. 10, which is to the same effect.

fol. 6 recto, line 27.

(1 Hen. VII. c. 9, Rot. Parl. nu. 73.) The silk-trade, which subsequently formed the main business of the Mercers, is stated in Statute 33 Hen. VI. c. 5 to have been carried on by the "silk-women and throwsters," who, petitioning for that Act, pray "that the Lombards and other strangers may be hindered from importing wrought silk into the kingdom contrary to custom, and to the ruin of the mystery and occupation of silk-making and other virtuous female occupations."

fol. 6 verso, line 9.

fol. 6 verso, line 27.

Wge or doo his lawe. This consisted in swearing upon the book that what the plaintiff stated was false. This oath had to be substantiated by six, eight, or twelve men, who attested the same, and were called compurgators. The offer to do this was named "wager of law," and to proceed in this manner was styled "doing of your law." The principal had to affirm directly the contrary of what was imputed to him, but the others merely swore that they believed that he spoke the truth. It was of no avail, however, against the King, nor was it permitted where the Plaintiff relied upon a deed, or other specialty, nor to an outlawed Defendant, or to one under 21 years of age, nor where the Plaintiff was an Infant, but it was permitted to a feme covert with her husband. In doing his law, he that waged his law, after being admonished by the judges of the nature and danger of a false oath repeated a form of oath denying the subject matter wherewith he was charged, and then eleven of his neighbours acting as compurgatory, avowed upon their oaths their belief that he spoke the Truth. The custom prevailed in the old Gothic constitution.

fol. 6 verso, line 18.

Essoyne, a plea for delay and non-appearance by reason of sickness or other just cause of absence. Five kinds of legal essoins are given in " *les Termes de la Ley* " (1641, p. 146). 1st, *essoin de ouster le mer,* by which forty days were granted. 2nd, *de terra sancta,* which lasted for a year and a day. 3rd, *de male vener,* or the common essoin, by which the suit was adjourned to a common day. 4th, *de malo lecti,* on account of sickness, for a year and a day. 5th, *service del Rey,* when the warrant had to be shown on the day, and a future date was appointed.

fol. 7 recto, line 18.

(1 Hen. VII. Rot. Parl. nu. 20.) As Bacon observes, it is evident by this statute that, " from the beginning, the King was not forgetful of his coffers, by drawing to himself the seizures and compositions of Italian goods, for not employment, being points of profit to his coffers."

fol. 8 recto, line 10.

Oost, the words of the Text at this reference are that "noo straüger of what coûtrey so euer shoolde oost or take to soiourne with him wythin this reame of Englond, ony marchaüte straüger not beyng of the same nacion that he sholde be of, upon peyné, &c." This prohibition seems to be twofold ; first against oosting the particular persons described, secondly, against taking them to sojourn : the meaning of the word oost is to be gathered from the act 18th, Henry VI., ch. IV., which enacts "that all merchant aliens and strangers, from henceforth coming and abiding to Merchandyse within any city, town, boro', or port in England, shall be under the surveying of certeyn people, to be called Hosts, or surveyors, to them assigned by the Mayor, Sheriffs, or Bailiffs, of the same cities, towns, boroughs, or ports." These Hosts were to be privy to all sales and contracts of aliens : their fee to be 2d. in every 20s. Merchandize bought or sold : Hosts to be sworn, and to be displaced for misconduct : Merchants of the Hanse towns were exempted from the requirement of this enactment.

xl. li. The founders of our legal polity, whenever they have had occassion to fix a certain number, have shown a strong predilection for the number forty. By the laws of Æthelberth, one of our Saxon Kings, the term for the payment of blood-money was fixed to 40 nights. At Preston, in the reign of Henry III., every newly-made burgess was compelled to build himself a house within 40 days, or he was mulcted 40 pence. Merchants from Lorrain anciently were only allowed to remain 40 days in the City, and in still older times no man was suffered to abide in England above 40 days unless he were enrolled in some tithing. A widow might remain in her husband's capital messuage for a term of 40 days. A tenure of a knight's service consisted in attending the King fully equipped for war yearly for 40 days. Those who took sanctuary were there in security for 40 days, and if they undertook to leave the country, 40 days more were granted them in order to effect this purpose. Members of Parliament were protected from arrest 40 days after prorogation and 40 days before the next meeting,

fol. 8 recto, line 14.

Persons coming from places in which epidemical sicknesses were prevalent had formerly to remain on board ship for 40 days, and hence the term *quarantine.* Nor is this preference for the number 40 confined to time only. A revenue of 40s. of land constituted a yeoman, who was anciently thereby qualified to vote for knights of the shire and serve on juries ; 40s. used to be the qualification of a freeholder at an election ; 40s. was anciently the limited value for causes in the County Court, the Court Baron, etc.; 40 was the original number of Knights of the Garter,

fol. 8 recto, line 20.

Carckes, carracks, or carracas, was the name given to a class of trading vessels. Ducange quotes mention of them occurring so early as 1342—Richard of Walsingham says that carrikes brought spices and wines to Southampton; and states also that in the reign of Henry V., the French, with the intention of molesting England, collected a fleet of large ships, carrikes and gallies.

fol. 8 recto, line 21.

Clakked or barbed wolle. To *clack* wool was the term for cutting off the sheep's mark, which caused it to weigh less and so to pay less customs. To *barb*, or rather *bard* or *beard* it, was to cut the head and neck from the fleece, for the same reason.

fol. 8 recto, line 21.

Lockes was what we now call Flock, from Lat. Floccus, a lock of wool ; Junius has "Lock, Tomentum, Floccus, Cirrus; Flock of wool, flocus Lanæ ;" Johnson has " Flock, a lock of wool ;" refuse, French *loque,* a rag or tatter.

fol. 8 verso, line 21.

The second parliament was called by writs bearing date September 1st, 1488, to meet at Westminster on the 9th November following.

fol. 8 verso, line 25.

(3 Hen. VII. c. 1, Rot. Parl. 17.)

Annotations.

Embrasaries. An attempt to influence a jury corruptly ;
severely punishable by fine and imprisonment under several
ancient statutes, and lately by Act 6, Geo. 4, c. 50, s. 61.
"When one laboreth the jury, if it be but to appear, or if he
instruct them, or put them in fear, or the like, it is a maintenance, and he is called in law an embraceor, and an action
of maintenance lyeth against him ; and if he takes money, a
decies tantum may be brought against him. And whether
the jury passe for his side or no, or whether the jury give
any verdict at all, yet shall he be punished as a maintainer
or embraceor, either at the suit of the king or partie."—
Coke upon Littleton.

fol. 9 recto, line 3.

Gayoll, old French gaol.

fol. 10 recto, line 12.

Batell by the cours of the comen lawe, etc. Trial by
battle, which might be chosen by the defendant in appeals
of murder, robbery, felony, and in suits of right ; long since
repealed.

fol. 10 verso, line 13.

(3 Hen. VII. c. 2, Rot. Parl. nu. 18.)

fol. 11 verso, line 23.

(3 Hen. VII. c. 3, Rot. Parl. nu. 24.)

fol. 11 recto, line 20.

Maynprice, maynprenable. Receiving a man into friendly
custody who otherwise might have been committed to
prison, giving security for his appearance on a day assigned.
Those that thus remained responsible were named *main-
pernours,* and the person taken into their custody were said
to be *mainpernable.*

fol. 11 verso, line 28.

Wythin franchies as wythout. The Franchise intended
here is a bailiwick or liberty exempt from the sheriff of the
county, wherein the grantee only and his officers are to
execute all process. Bl. Com : B. II., 37.

fol. 12 recto, line 11.

Oon, one.

fol. 12 verso, line 3.

(3 Hen. VII. c. 4, Rot. Parl. nu. 20.)

fol. 12 verso, line 5.

fol. 12 verso, line 20.   (3 Hen. VII, c. 6, Rot. Parl. nu. 29.)

fol. 12 verso, line 23.   *Cheuysauce.* An agreement or composition particularly between debtor and creditor. It was also used in the meaning of interest, or what was synonymous with that according to the ideas of the time, usury. Thus, in the Paston Letters (XLVIII. vol. iv. p. 173): "two hundred marks to be lent unto you for an half year, without any *chevisance.*" . . .

fol. 13 recto, line 5.   *Loue,* error in original for *lone,* loan.

fol. 13 verso, line 18.   *Reserwyng to the chyrche,* etc. Thus, Statute 15 Edw. II. c. v.: "Item, it is accorded and assented that the King and his heirs shall have the cognizance of the userers dead, and the ordinaries of the Holy Church have the cognizance of the usurers on life, as to them apperteineth to make compulsion by the censures of Holy Church for the sin, to make restitution of the usuries taken against the laws of Holy Church."

fol. 13 verso, line 21.   (3 Hen. VII. c. 7, Rot. Parl. nu. 28.) In order to put into circulation the money coined at the mints, exchanges were appointed in various places from whence the newly-formed coins were issued, and in which bullion was purchased for the supply of the mint. At a very early period the exclusive privilege of purchasing precious metals was claimed by our monarchs, who appointed proper officers to whom they delegated that branch of their prerogative. The duty of these officers was not only to exchange the current coins of one metal for those made of another, but also to receive wrought silver, plate and bullion, and foreign coins, according to their fineness respectively ; and as the exportation of coin of the realm was prohibited, they furnished persons going out of the kingdom with foreign coin in exchange for English, and also supplied merchant strangers coming into the kingdom with English coins in exchange for foreign. These exchanges were regulated by a table, which was hung up in the exchanger's office.

In the fiftene yere of Kynge Edwarde, etc. Errata are numerous in this collection, but at this place the old compositor has been particularly careless, for not only has he put fifteenth for twenty-fifth, but he has also left out some lines, as appears from other sources, where the statute reads as follows: "In the twentie fifth yere of Kynge Edwarde the thyrde ch. 12, and a oder espall statute made in 'the V^t year of Richarde the ij^{de} with oder dyvse statutes made for the same reamedy in," etc.

Such as the Kynge shall depute. On the accession of Henry VII., two persons were appointed to this office for ten years, at an annual fee of £30 6s. 8d., viz., Richard Fox and William Stafford. Richard Fox subsequently, as Bishop of Winchester, played a prominent part in this and the following reign. In 1509 Peter Corsy, merchant of Florence, was appointed to this office, "the said Peter to conduct all foreign exchanges and rechanges at the rate of 3d. for the exchange and rechange of each ducat of gold, over and above 1d., which used to be paid for the same." Ruding, Annals of the Coinage, vol. iv., p. 160.

^{1} (3 Hen. VII. c. 8, Rot. Parl. nu. 33.)

Wered, Valued, from the Anglo-Saxon weorth, wurth, wyrth; worth, price, value, in L. 1 Edouardi confessoris c. II. legitur, Were suum, id est pretium suæ redemptionis.

Vesses rayes sayling clothes. Sometimes, instead of vesses, we read vesset, and in some copies of this Act the word is spelled vesseis: whatever colour it was (perhaps the colour of the vetch blossom), it was formerly much in use. Rayes cloth is probably the same as cloth of ray, striped or rayed cloth, in mediæval Latin, *pannus radiatus.* Mention of a "ray gown" is made in the Paston Letters (CI., vol. iv., p. 421); where it is explained as "a gown made of cloth that was never either coloured or dijed." Cloth of say is a kind of serge.

fol. 13 verso, line 30.

fol. 14 recto, line 7.

fol. 14 verso, line 6.

fol. 14 verso, line 28.

fol. 18 recto, line 23.

fol. 18 recto, line 25.

(3 Hen. VII. c. 15, Rot. Parl. 23.)

fol. 18 recto, line 30.

Chaces, parkes, and warens. The difference between these three is, that the *park* is an enclosed space in which game is kept ; the *chase* is larger, and not enclosed, and differs from a forest in this, that the chase may belong to a subject. A *warren* is a place privileged by prescription or grant of the King for the preservation of hares, rabbits, partridges, and pheasants.

fol. 18 recto, line 13.

Vert, In the forest laws, was everything within the forest that grows and bears a green leaf. *Over vert* were the large trees, *under vert* the underwood. Trees that bear fruit upon which the deer feed were called *special vert*, and the destruction of these was more severely punished than that of the other verts. A ballad of the early part of the 13th century begins thus :

       " Sumer is ycumen,
           &c.,
        Bulluc sterteth,
        Buck verteth.

from A.-S., a leap. Chaucer uses sterting, in the sense of leaping nimbly.

fol. 18 verso, line 18.

In his grete troubles, Alluding to the insurrection of Lovel and the Staffords, the Lambert Simnel conspiracy and the revolt in Ireland on that occasion.

fol. 19 verso, line 2.

Dibdin considers this article on the price of long-bows to be a chapter with the title omitted, which it obviously is ; the statute passed in the third Parliament of the king, regulating the price of cloth, is also without a title.

fol. 19 recto, line 13.

Conysauce. The badge or cognisance was the master's crest, supporter of his arms, or other heraldic emblem, worn in the cap or on the chest. Thus Henry's cognisances were the dragon, the greyhound, the hawthorn-tree, the portcullis, the falcon and fetterlock, the combined red and white rose, etc.

(3 Hen VII. c. 13, Rot. Parl. nu. 31.)

fol. 19 verso, line 1.

(3 Hen. VII. c. 14, Rot. Parl. nu. 26.)

fol. 19 verso, line 19.

As now late, viz., in the Simnel conspiracy, which it was thought had been fostered and countenanced by the Queen Dowager, and in which John Earl of Lincoln and several other nobles had been deeply implicated.

fol. 19 verso, line 28.

Sad and discrete psones. Sad, in old English, was synony-mous with serious: "My father and the gentleman are in sad talk," Winter's Tale, iv. 3 ; also in Roger Ascham's Schoolmaster, p. 27 : " Rather than for anything in it which should helpe good sad studye."

fol. 20 recto, line 10.

Exspiratur. (3 Hen. VII. c. 16, Rot. Parl. nu. 22.) This Act in Rot. Parl. is entitled, "An Act to enable feoffes in trust to sue for y^e benefytt of y^e Feffors although they be outlawed."

fol. 20 verse, line 1.

At the end of the fourth year 148$^5_6$ the King called his third parliament, but the express time is not mentioned in Dugdale, for the summons to this parliament was not to be found on the roll. However, the statute-books say it began 13 Jan. 148$^5_6$, and was, on the 23rd of February following, prorogued to 14th October, 1489, or 5 Hen. VII., in which session were passed the Acts numbered chap. 1 to 7 of the Statutes. On the said 14th of October the parliament met, and sat until 14th December following, and was then pro-rogued to January 25 ensuing, 14$^{89}_{90}$, in which session were passed the two Acts numbered chap. 8 and 9 of the Statutes. And on the said 25th of January the parliament met, and sat until 27th February following (5 Hen. VII.), 14$^{89}_{90}$, and

fol. 21 recto, line 1.

was then dissolved, in which session were passed the Acts numbered chap. 10 to 24. The whole of these Statutes is always cited as 4 Hen. 7. It was not until the year 1752 that the new computation came into use in England, by the adoption of the Gregorian method, although it had long prevailed in Italy, Spain, Portugal, and Switzerland, Germany, and Holland, Russia still maintains the Julian style : when the old style prevailed in England, the year commenced on the 24th March, hence the reason of subsequently writing any date on or after the 1st June, or before the 24th March, 170$\frac{8}{9}$, meaning the year 1709 according to the new style, the year 1708 according to the old style.

fol. 21 recto, line 11.

(4 Hen. VII. c. 1, Rot. Parl. nu. 19.)

fol. 21 verso, line 2.

(4 Hen. VII. c. 2, Rot. Parl. nu. 20). *Fvnours,* refiners of gold and silver.

fol. 21 verso, line 7.

London, Calays, Canterbery, York, and Durham. These five towns, with Dublin, appear at that period to have been the only places in the British dominions possessed of mints ; no British coins have been found struck in other towns during this reign.

fol. 22 recto, line 23.

Sterling. Birche, Hist. liv. : derives this term from the city of Stirling in Scotland, where he thinks sterling money was first struck. Vossius derives it from Easterling, Oosterling, a Dane. N. Bailey says that the Easterlings, Prussians and Pomeranians, in old times were artists in fining gold and silver, and taught it to the Britons ; Camden in his remains says that in the time of Richard 1st. money coined in the East part of Germany began to be of special request in England, for its purity, and was called Easterling money, as the inhabitants of these parts were called Easterlings : shortly some of that country, skilful in Mint matters and Allayes were sent for hither, to bring over coin to perfection, which since that time was called from them Sterling or Easterling.

Amelles, French *émails,* enamels ; thus, in Fletcher's
Purple Island, x., 33 :

    " Heaven's richest diamonds set in amel white ;"
and in the " Dutchess of Suffolk," a. iv.
        " A husband like an ammell would enrich
      Your golden virtues."

(4 Hen. VII. c. 3, Rot. Parl. 21.)

Saynt Gregories. This church stood at the south-west
corner of St. Paul's Churchyard. It was one of the oldest
churches of London, having probably been erected soon
after the foundation of St. Paul's Cathedral.

Slaughter of bestes. By a statute of 21 Edw. III. it was
enacted that all cattle for the consumption of London
should be killed either at the town of Knightsbridge or
the town of Stratford, and that their intestines be there
cleaned, and, together with the flesh, brought to town.
From the preamble to that Act it would appear that, before
that time, the blood of the animals that were killed in London was allowed to run down the streets, and that the offal
was cast into the Thames. Things evidently had come to
almost as bad a predicament in the reign of Henry VII.
In the Rate-books of St. Martin's in the Fields, Westminster, frequent mention is made in the 17th century of "the
Neat houses at Knightsbridge ;" they are also mentioned
by Dodsley, in his London and its Environs, and Nares says
they remained within his recollection on the same spot.

Bocherie of Seynt Nycholas Flesshamels. St. Nicholas
Fleshamels was a church in or near Newgate Street, pulled
down at the time of the Reformation. It derived its name
from the shambles or butchery near which it was situated.
The amenities of the neighbourhood are further illustrated
by the old and expressive name of King Edward Street,
which Stow informs us was anciently called " Stinking
Lane."

fol. 24 verso, line 2. *The palays where the Kynges moost royal person*, etc. The Bishop of London's palace, the name of which survives in that of London House Yard. It perished in the Great Fire, and on the site of it were built the houses now standing between the yard just mentioned and the present Chapter House. The Bishop's palace was often used for the reception of princes. Edward III. and his Queen were entertained there after a great tournament in Smithfield, and Edward V. lodged in it previous to his appointed coronation.

fol. 24 verso, line 13. (4 Hen. VII. c. 4, Rot. Parl. nu. 17.) Henry was at this time preparing an expedition into Brittany, which had been invaded by Charles VIII. of France, and, much against his will, was forced to appear to go along with the public opinion of England, and prevent the annexation of that dukedom to France. Accordingly, in the spring of 1489, a small force proceeded to Brittany, under command of Lord Willoughby of Broke.

fol. 24 verso, line 23. *Emysson of Assizes.* Assise was a writ which lay where a man was put out of his lands, tenements, or any profit to be made in a certain place, and so disseised of his freehold, abolished by 3 and 4 W. IV., c. 27. "If a man which hath a rent secke, be once seized of any parsel of the rent, and after the Tenant will not pay the rent behind, this is his remedie." "And of such disseisins he may have an assize of novel disseisin against the tenant, and shall recover the seisin of the rent, and his arrerages, and his damages, and the costs of his writ, and of his plea," &c. *Coke upon Litt.* "Assisa properly cometh of the word assideo, to sit together, so as probably assize is an Association, or sitting together, and the writ whereby certain persons are called together, is called Assisa Novæ disseisinæ, so as assize is but cessio." (Sessio).

fol. 24 verso, line 27. *Nouel dissesin as of fressheforce.* Novel disseisin is when the disseisor is dispossessed again by the person he had disseised. *Fressheforce* is a force committed by disseisement, abatement, intrusion of any land or tenement. For the redressing of this wrong he that had right might have his remedy without writ by an assise or bill of fressheforce, brought within forty days after the force committed or title to him accrued, in which action he could make his protestation to sue in the nature of what writ he liked.

(4 Hen. VII. c. 5, Rot. Parl. nu. 19.)   fol. 25 verso, line 29.

On the enrolment of this Act after the royal assent, provisions in favour of numerous abbots were inserted. At the head of these are the Dean of Windsor and the Abbot of Westminster. See Statutes of the Realm, p. 530.   fol. 26 recto, line 20.

(4 Hen. VII. c. 6, Rot. Parl. nu. 15. Inglewood or Englewood. William the Conqueror having dispossessed the Scotch of the County of Cumberland, gave it to Ranulph de Meschiens, one of his Norman followers. He reserved, however, for his own use a large tract in the middle of the county, between the eastern and western mountains, covered with forest, and full of red and fallow deer, wild boars, and all kinds of game. This was the forest of Englewood, which lay between the rivers of Shawk and Eden ; it extended from Carlisle to Penrith, and covered a surface of sixteen miles in length by ten miles in breadth. See the boundaries as taken in a perambulation, 29 Edw. I., in Nicholson and Burn's History and Antiquities of Westmoreland and Cumberland, Vol. II., p. 522.   fol. 26 recto, line 21.

Thomas Lord Dacre of Gillisland was warden of the Westmarches. He died October 25th, 1525. The title became dormant by the attainder of Leonard Lord Dacre in 1569, for participation in the rebellion of the Earls of Northumberland and Westmoreland.   fol. 26 verso, line 2.

· · *Earl of Northumbr̄.* Henry Percy, fourth Earl of Northumberland, who was in great favour with Henry VII. on   fol. 26 verso, line 7.

account of his having remained neutral at the battle of
Bosworth, keeping his numerous forces of Northern men
from joining in the battle, which materially contributed to
the overthrow of Richard III. Henry made him Lord
Lieutenant of Northumberland ; he was murdered by the
revolted North Country men 28th April, 1489. Skelton, in
his quality of Poet Laureate, wrote an elegy on the earl's
death.

fol. 16 verso, line 9. Three other provisions are entered on the enrolment of
this Act, after the royal assent, in favour of Walter Story,
William Walton, and Richard Brown, Foresters.

fol. 26 verso, line 10. (4 Hen. VII. c. 7., Rot. Parl. nu. 13.)

fol. 16 verso, line 15. (4 Hen. VII. c. 8, Rot. Parl. nu. 25.)

fol. 27 recto, line 20. *Saynte Thomas the Appostell*, December 21. Bacon
much admired "the wise model of this Act, not prescribing
prices, but stinting them not to exceed a rate, that the
clothier might drape accordingly as he might afford."

fol. 27 recto, line 23. (4 Hen. VII. c. 9, Rot. Parl. nu. 24.)

fol. 28 verso, line 21. (4 Hen. VII. c. 10, Rot. Parl. nu. 39.) *Tolowse wood*, i.e.,
woad, a plant used as a blue dye before the introduction of
indigo, but since completely abandoned, the indigo being
much cheaper. The wild woad (French, *vaud*) was and is
still used as a yellow dye. This statute is a repetition and
enlargement of 1 Hen. VII. c. 8, the preamble being almost
literally the same.

fol. 28 verso, line 16. (4 Hen. VII. c. 11, Rot. Parl. nu. 40.)

fol. 29 verso, line 4. (4 Hen. VII. c. 12, Rot. Parl. nu. 41.)

fol. 30 recto, line 3. *Exchetours. Escheat.* It was when a tenant in fee simple
had committed any felony for which he was hanged, or when

he had abjured the realm, or been outlawed; or if a tenant died without heir, then the lord of whom he held the land was allowed to enter by way of *escheat*, or if another took possession, the lord could have a writ against him of *escheat*. From this term was derived the word *escheator*, the title of an officer whose duty it was to observe the *escheats* in the county of which he was *escheator*, and notify them to the Exchequer. The escheater was appointed by letters patent from the Lord Treasurer, and the office was anxiously sought after, whence it may be inferred that it was profitable, his inquests were to be taken by good and lawful men of the county, impanelled by the Sheriff. *4th Inst.* 225.

(4 Hen. VII. c. 13. Rot. Parl. nu. 42.) Benefit of Clergy was originally strictly confined to those having the *habitum et tonsuram clericalem*, but in process of time, every one who could [show] a mark of great learning in those days came to be accounted a Clerk or Clericus, and was admitted to the privilegium clericale; this stat. was passed in order to draw a distinction between lay scholars and clerks in orders, accordingly it directs that no person once admitted to the benefit of clergy, shall be admitted thereto a second time unless he produces his orders, and in order to distinguish their persons, all laymen admitted to this privilege are to be burnt with a hot iron, in the brawn of the left thumb.

The neck verse. After the offender had delivered his neck-verse, he was finally delivered over to the Ordinary, to be dealt with according to the ecclesiastical canons, and to make purgation by undergoing the form of a canonical trial. This second trial took place before the bishop or his deputy, and a jury of twelve persons who gave their verdict on oath; the prisoner answered on oath, the witnesses were examined on oath, and twelve compurgators affirmed on oath that they believed him. On this, though the prisoner had been convicted at common law by the clearest evidence, or had even confessed his guilt, he was invariably acquitted: the neck verse was generally the first verse of the 31st Psalm (the Miserere) in a Latin MS. Psalter: but it was not always that particular verse, a more difficult one might be assigned. Otway has "He cant write his name nor read his neckverse."

fol. 31 recto, line 6. (4 Hen. VII. c. 14, Rot. Parl. nu. 43.) Edward Plantagenet, son of Edward IV., had been the last Earl of March. When he succeeded to the Crown in 1483, as Edward Vth, all his previous titles were merged in the kingly dignity. The title was not derived from any city or county.

fol. 31 verso, line 18. (4 Hen. VII. c. 15, Rot. Parl. nu. 44.)

fol. 31 verso, line 31. *From the brydge of Stanys*, etc. The jurisdiction of the Lord Mayor and Corporation of London extends from Colneditch above Staines bridge in the West, to the Yenlet, or, as it is called in old deeds, Yenland versus Mare, in the East, and includes part of the rivers Lea and Medway.

fol. 32 recto, line 20. *Groūde soo drowned.* Not only the water, with the fish therein, belongs to the City, but also the soil and ground of it, as appears from the following memorandum found among the manuscripts of Burleigh, Lord Treasurer in the reign of Queen Elizabeth :—"Also for proof of the Prince's interest in rivers flowing from the sea, the Thames and conservation thereof was not only given to the City of London, but, by their special suit, the King gave therewithal the ground and soil under the same: whereupon, if any that has a house or land adjoining do make a strand, stairs, or such like, they pay forthwith a rent to the City of London, how high soever they be above the low-watermark."

fol. 33 recto, line 26. *Marlcbridge, i.e.,* Marlborough. Henry III., in 1269, held a Parliament at Marlborough, in which were made what were called the Statutes of Malbridge. They may be said to have formed an appendix to Magna Charta.

Releef, an incident to knight's service, was a certain sum of money which the heir had to pay to the lord of whom those lands were held, which, after the decease of his ancestor, descended to him. The relief of a whole knight's fee was one hundred shillings.

fol. 33 verso, line 24.

Wast, for Waste, is where a tenant for life or for term of years or a guardian in chevalry doth, to the prejudice of the heir, or of him in the reversion, make waste or spoil of houses, woods, gardens, orchards, etc., by pulling down the house, cutting the timber, etc.

fol. 33 verso, line 29.

(4 Hen. VII. c. 19, Rot. Parl. nu. 48.) In the Statutes of the Realm this Act is entitled, "An Act agaynst pullyng down of townes."

fol. 34 recto, line 25.

Halfendele, A.-S. Half part: dele or deel, part. From A.-S. deel or dele, a part, from deelan to divide: this word survives in our day, in the verb deal, as to deal the cards, to divide them into parts amongst the players; and as a noun substantive in the ordinary phrase—a good deal, a great deal.

fol. 35 recto, line 8.

(4 Hen. VII. c. 20, Rot. Parl. nu. 49.) *Accions Populers.* An action popular was an action given upon the breach of some penal statute, the which action every man that would might sue for himself and the King, by information or otherwise, as the Statute allowed and the case required.—

fol. 35 recto, line 21.

Mayntenaūces. Many Statutes were passed against the offence of Maintenance.

fol. 35 recto, line 24.

Couyn, covin. A conspiracy between two or more, to the prejudice of another. Covina cometh of the French word convisie, and is a secret assent determined in the hearts of two or more, to the defrauding and prejudice of another.

fol. 35 recto, line 30.

fol. 36 recto, line 3. *Abarre,* aver.

fol. 36 recto, line 16. *Capias utlagat.* This was a writ in outlawry directing the sheriff to take, utlagatum, the outlaw ; from A.-S. ut lage, out of law.

fol. 36 verso, line 2. (4 Hen. VII. c. 21, Rot. Parl. nu. 50.) Orford was formerly a place of considerable traffic and importance, so as to have been able, in 1359, to send vessels and troops to the siege of Calais. But the sea retiring, and throwing up a dangerous bar at the mouth of the river, choked up the harbour, so that the trade and fishery fell to decay, and with them the town became deserted.

fol. 37 recto, line 1. (4 Hen. VII. c. 22, Rot. Parl. nu. 51.) *Brouderers,* embroiderers.

fol .37 recto, line 1. *Jeane,* Genoa.

fol. 37 verso, line 2. *Vntrue packyng.* The complaint was, that the trundles or quills of gold thread imported from Italy were deficient in weight, and made up of an inferior quality of gold thread, with a layer of superior thread over the surface, so as to deceive the purchaser.

fol. 38 recto, line 21. *Kyng henri the vij.* Error in original for Henry VI. The " persones as ben dispensed " were those who paid ransoms for English prisoners beyond the sea ; soldiers were also allowed to take a reasonable amount of money with them when sent on expeditions into foreign countries, and the inhabitants of the northern counties were allowed to pay English money for cattle bought in Scotland. (2 Hen. VI. c. 6.)

fol. 38 verso, line 7. *Nota de Finibus.* Coke describes a fine as a final agreement which was used to put an end to suits, and says that it was made with the consent of the king, or his justices ; but a note in Hargrave's edition of Coke upon Litt. says, " this gives a very inadequate idea of fines : in Glanville's time they were really amicable compositions of actual suits, but for several centuries past they have been so only in name, being in fact fictitious proceedings, in order to transfer or secure real property, by a mode more efficacious than ordinary conveyances : another use of them was to bar estates tail : the subject involves much abstruse learning." The object of this act was to ensure perfect publicity to the levying of fines, by causing them to be proclaimed in open court, on four several days in term time, and when so levied to bar all adverse claims to the lands, &c., unless prosecuted within the time prescribed by the Act. In 1833 the Act 3-4, Wm. IV., c. 74, was passed " for the abolition of fines and recoveries."

Yefte, gift.   fol. 39 verso, line 17.

Couert de baron. A married woman is styled in law a   fol. 39 verso, line 27.
femme covert. Baron is Norman French for a husband, from the Spanish word *varo,* a man.   *Vncouert,* which occurs a few lines lower, has of course a meaning opposed to covert.

INDEX.